AMANDA DOBRA HOPE

The Healing of the Masculine and Feminine

How to Truly Change the World From the Inside, Out

First published by Golden Dolphin Publishing 2020

First edition

ISBN: 978-0-578-63760-0

Cover art by Greg Troyan II- Cover Design
Cover art by H.N. James- Punk Rock Photography, Nashville, TN- Author Photo

This book was professionally typeset on Reedsy.
Find out more at reedsy.com

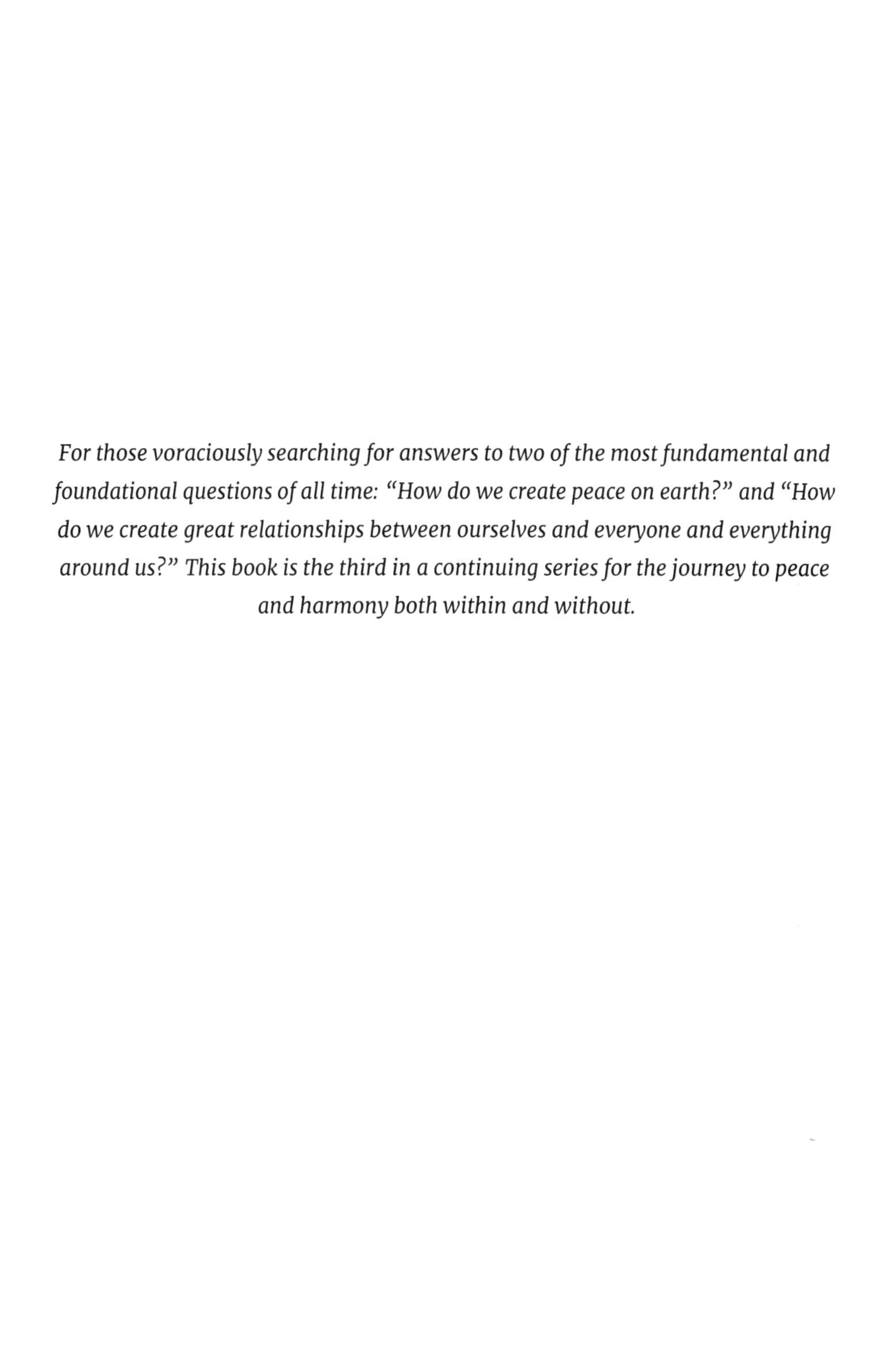

For those voraciously searching for answers to two of the most fundamental and foundational questions of all time: "How do we create peace on earth?" and "How do we create great relationships between ourselves and everyone and everything around us?" This book is the third in a continuing series for the journey to peace and harmony both within and without.

Foreword

Growing up I was taught that men are only to work, make money, and dominate everything and everyone in order to reach high rank in anything. Like most males I was told "men don't cry." The message was often conveyed with aggression, and sometimes with screaming. Though I now understand that the guidelines my early teachers provided me were half-truths about survival and suppressing tears, I also understand that these teachings had been passed down from generation to generation. Though their rules were misleading to the soul's purpose, I can appreciate their effort as their intentions were good.

The truth is that when we tell our young boys "men don't cry" it dispels their emotions and creates an imbalance of the masculine and feminine energies from within. It also makes it difficult for them to receive love or explore different forms of spirituality.

That is what happened to me. Last year, I was battling with loneliness. I felt completely absent from myself, my friends, and my family. There was a void inside of me that I couldn't figure out—all I knew was that it needed to be filled. I tried to fill it in a most detrimental way by not eating, trapping myself in a dark room away from people, and being verbally aggressive to myself and others. I believe I was searching for connection in an indirect way, but it became an unhealthy cycle that scared me. One morning while I was staring at the ceiling I prayed to my higher power. I said, "God, use me. I surrender. Heaven save me."

After that prayer that I decided to move in the direction of authenticity and align myself with soul. Along the journey toward the soul, complete with the baggage of trauma, I met my good friend Amanda Dobra Hope. Her teachings about relationships, holding space, and authenticity have inspired me to connect with myself and others on a deep level. For so long I've been afraid of connection because I felt ashamed of my emotions, while at the same time, I knew that I needed to explore them. I so desperately wanted to express my feelings.

I believe we all want to experience a deep connection (to be seen, heard, and felt) with ourselves, friends, nature, and family. I realize we are called into this life to experience oneness and abundance, not the separation and fear that our cultural norms have encouraged. Amanda has taught me that in order to create any change in this world I must start with myself. If I want to create love and connection in this world, I must practice love and connection with myself. I believe this to be true because I believe that heaven we seek lives in our hearts. If I tap into that feminine part of my being, and balance it with the masculine—then like alchemy, fears transmute into love.

Tavarus Williams- Future Humanitarian

Acknowledgement

Special thank you to the supporters of this book: Greg Troyan, Tavarus Williams, Kerry Norman, Nancy Ingraham, Megan Laubenheimer, H.N. James (punkrockphotography.net); Jonathan Stone-check out his business at-(jonathanstonearts.com), *Marcus Guillory- check out his business at- (Shift Your Perspective Studios), and so many more for your: love, support, financial and in-kind donations, and belief in my work.*

Table of Contents

Preface

This aim of this book is to examine the role the imbalance of the masculine and feminine as energies/concepts has played in the conundrum of relationship and separation from Source and others. I will look at the masculine and feminine through three lenses in order to illustrate this point. The lenses are: the divine masculine and feminine within each of us, the physiological and character traits we wear as embodied males or females, and the cultural norms of being considered male or female. As we bring these things forth to be examined, I believe we can begin to look at where our actions have brought us closer to oneness, and where we have fallen further into duality by ignoring the balance necessary between the masculine and feminine in all respects. This book will provide evidence of how healing our world from the inside will then radiate out, leading to a lighter, care-free, and more authentic life for all of us on the global stage—a life in which all beings can share equally, co-create in freedom, and stand side by side in support and love. Essentially—heaven on earth! Just imagine all of the possibilities for our unlimited human creative potential in this state of being!

The Three Lenses

Masculine and Feminine Energies (The Divine Masculine and Divine Feminine)

Masculine and feminine energies exist inside of all of us as well as everywhere we look in our world. To refer to the masculine and feminine energies does not mean we are referring to men or women, it means we are referring to the traits carried by each energy. In order to function in wholeness within ourselves and within the world we live in, our masculine and feminine energies must be balanced.

Masculine energies include things such as: doing, structure, rules, plans, academia, action steps, and making things tangible. Feminine energies include things like: being, relationships, allowing things time to gestate (holding space), entering into the creative field, spirituality, and allowing. Because this entire book will cover what it means to use these energies and how they must be utilized for the best results, I will leave this definition open-ended for now.

Gender- The Physiological Embodiment of the Masculine and Feminine

If you identify with and are physically male, you are the physiological embodiment of the masculine. This means that you carry the physical presence of masculine genes, etc., but also that you naturally lean a bit toward the masculine energies of order, logic, reason, action, etc. This is a general statement of course, but it will help greatly in the unraveling of the wounds of the masculine and feminine.

The same is true if you are a woman, meaning that you are the physiological embodiment of the feminine, and therefore also naturally embody more feminine energies. Females seem to quite naturally be more in tune with their intuition, relationships, holding space, etc. than the other genders. It is theorized that because a woman's monthly menstrual cycle and her ability to give birth coincide with natural cycles (i.e. moon phases, etc.), they naturally cause her to then be more attuned with those energies.

Perhaps those in generations past have been perfectly happy with keeping the men in one role and women in another, but in the cycle of the grand experiment we currently live within, the quest is to learn to embody and harmonize both sides, while still having a slight lean to the side you are embodied in (just as we all have certain traits we are more heavily talented in or tuned in to). As you will see throughout this book, both sides are needed, and it is part of our personal and collective growth to cultivate them both in our inner world as well as our outer world.

In a book such as this, in a section such as this, we must also look at the LGBTQ community. I have a theory that this community may be exactly where we need to look to understand nature's need to balance itself. Perhaps those that physiologically or emotionally embody either more of the opposite gender than their own, or both, are naturally this way in order to bring that balance. If we weren't quite ready to understand how to balance the polarities of masculine and feminine, nature would take care of it for us—but that's another book. The point is that a balancing of the masculine and feminine, and therefore a return to more androgyny in our beings and behaviors, may be exactly what is called for if we wish to evolve past the heaviness of duality, and into a higher consciousness fueled by love, connection, and nurturing for ourselves and everything around us. Instead of ostracizing or shunning those who either don't identify with their embodied gender, or perhaps don't identify with either gender, perhaps the rest of us should thank them for showing us the way.

How Our Culture Influences Acceptable Behavior Based on Physical Gender

From our infancy, no matter what culture we live in, we are all influenced by a myriad of written and unwritten, spoken and unspoken rules for our gender. In the Western world, men have been told to suppress their feminine sides and "man up," and women have long been told to suppress their masculine sides by being "seen and not heard." In recent modern culture (since the dawn of television and modern music and media), men have been largely been portrayed either as aggressive and dominating (in many aspects), or complete buffoons not to be trusted with anything (think old TV sitcoms). Women in these times have been depicted either as nagging know-it-alls, brainless arm candy, temptresses to be dominated, or completely submissive and needing direction from a man. All of these cultural norms have hurt us individually and as a society, and all of them are unhealthy in the forms in which they are being displayed.

Telling our boys to "man up" and that "boys don't cry," has completely split men off from their feminine sides, making it much more difficult for them to relate to women as they have trouble even relating to and knowing themselves (feminine energies). This has caused heartbreak across the genders, and has been passed on to the children in many cases. Scenes in television, movies, and media depicting men as dominators at all costs (with other men, in business, with women), has reduced them to appearing as competitive warring machines, fighting daily against the world and the people around them. These portrayals have taught the men that they must compete rather than cooperate, and that they'd better be the alpha of the pack if they want to "win" at life. The problem with this is that humans are highly intelligent creatures in a complex society. We have large brains. We are not meant to act as carnal animals who are only concerned for our own survival. Each of us acting as the "lone wolf" is not how we were designed to exist. Just like dolphins, elephants, chimpanzees, and whales (other highly intelligent animals), we were designed as a species that needs community and cooperation to exist. With the advancement of modern society, and the fact that we do not live in hunter/gatherer societies anymore for the most part, the playing field has been evened exponentially for males and females. We now have the capacity and capability (because we are not running from angry lions everyday) to fully develop our masculine and feminine sides. Teaching boys and men that they should continue to take power roles to the point of overpowering everything around them will not bring them the peace, community, and harmony in themselves and their families that they are seeking. Teaching them that women are submissive playthings to be dominated is violent and harmful for the women, while at the same time only depriving men of the key they truly need to achieve balance in their lives.

In order for men and women to enjoy deeper relationships with themselves and others and relate in peace and harmony to the world around them, they must learn to respect themselves. Movies, TV, and music depicting male domination over submissive oversexualized females are not helping that cause. Little boys and girls watching these things may grow up thinking that they need to act a certain way to "get" the girl or boy. This can cause them to act in ways that are unhealthy and disrespectful to both themselves and their future partners, as well as out of alignment with themselves. To be clear, I am not in any way suggesting that sexuality is bad and should be suppressed. What I am saying is that in order to create healthy, sustainable relationships with ourselves, our partners, and the world around us, we must base those relationships (starting with ourselves) on love, respect, cooperation, and healthy expressions of all of the earthly pleasures that exist for us. We must partake of them in ways that are sustainable and encouraging for ourselves and others, giving all parts of ourselves expression in ways that glean positive results in all areas. Allowing ourselves a chance to breathe and enjoy, but in a way that we are not destroying a stable, healthy foundation for ourselves, as well as everything and everyone around us in the meantime.

Introduction

The original fall into duality has been seen by some as the beginning of the grand experiment called life. No matter how you see it, the shift from oneness to separateness consciousness has played out in the continual struggle for balance as humans have gone from one end of the pendulum swing to the other. The struggle for balance, the shift toward equality, and the quest for the zero-point have shaped our world for eons on the big stage, as well as in our homes. Since the beginning of time, humans have attempted to harmonize and synergize themselves, only to end up in competition or conflict with one another and the environment that surrounds them. Divine masculine qualities of power, action, and direction have been allowed to become out of balance and have emerged in their unhealthy forms of control, force, and dominance. This has occurred due to the suppression of divine feminine qualities such as gestation, timing, right relations, and cooperation. For humans to fully enjoy the unlimited creative potential allotted to them during their life on earth while sustainably enjoying the fruits of their labors, both masculine and feminine properties must be allowed to synergize and harmonize, with the feminine being engaged first (more on that later). The main point for now is that both are necessary and needed parts of the whole.

Is it possible that the original fall into duality (symbolized here by the grand polarities of masculine and feminine) has left us fearful and distrustful of ourselves and each other, and out of touch with the state of grace, or Love, that is the key to our oneness as a universe? Has every story of creation and how it became divided into polarities been encoded into our DNA, forever affecting us—or is it possible to create our future consciously, by choosing to evolve past duality into oneness and harmony?

Perhaps the grand experiment was a test that ultimately left us to choose the world we wish to live in. Will we rise higher spiritually and accept, nurture, and love ourselves and our surroundings? I believe most of us care about our time on this planet and what we do with it. Perhaps it's time to look deeper and begin healing the root cause of our imbalance. For centuries, humans have attempted to ignite change from the outside, in. Many types of programs and groups have been formed to attempt to bring peace to large groups of people in every country, state, city, and community. Change has consistently been approached from the outside, using masculine principles of energy and creation. However, just as modern medicine has shown that it is far superior when treating a fracture or broken bone than addressing the root cause of disease or imbalance in the cells, perhaps to heal the emotional and spiritual wounds of our civilization, we must dig to find the core emotional issues. Therefore, rather than attempt the change from the outside in, or the macrocosm to the microcosm, I suggest that the healing start first individually, and ripple out from there.

Our spiritual quest for balance and overall synergizing of the masculine and feminine in all aspects cannot be achieved within our current societal consciousness. Philosophers and evolutionaries throughout the ages have pointed out that it is not possible to create solutions within the same consciousness the problem was created in. It is for this reason that we need to work less on looking for solutions to our existing emotional and relationship issues at the level of polarity and duality, and instead begin to create solutions in the higher vibrations of harmony and oneness. If energy can be directed towards emotional intelligence (discovering, processing, and transforming our feelings and emotions), in partnership with surrender to whatever benevolent force we believe is larger than us for guidance, we can transform ourselves and become better able to bear witness to others. These tools will allow us to move back into balance, and deliver us again into our natural state of oneness, cooperation, and co-creation with each other and all things. Healing ourselves and our intimate relationships can begin to form the sustainable roots needed to bring all walks of life together, and to allow the tree of life to grow in a way that will continue to last for many generations to come.

In order to do this, we must be willing to look into our thought patterns, beliefs, and cultural norms in order to find out how and why our relationships with others and our environment have become so unbalanced in the first place. The earth and its people are out of balance and we are at a crossroads. To begin our journey back to oneness, love, and grace, we must re-learn the divine feminine qualities of respect, humility, and reverence. The divine masculine qualities of forward motion, directed action, and power cannot continue to survive unbalanced.

It is my theory that people will not learn to respect the earth and all of its creatures until they can learn to respect themselves and remember their oneness in realizing that everything is a part of them, and that every aspect is an important part of the whole. Our children are growing up in our families. If we cannot heal ourselves and our intimate partnerships, we will send forth our children in the world in the same manner in which we ourselves have been accustomed. These children will then become the adults of the future, with the power again to make or break our world. We have the power to do the inner work. Let's break the pattern and rise as a society to build a world of creation and beauty, born from choice and personal responsibility to ourselves and our human family.

The original fall into duality made us hyper-aware of our differences, and for many eons, those differences were augmented as inadequacies, faults, and things to fight over—rather than pieces of the puzzle to be brought together. Combine that with each of our own imbalances in our inner masculine and feminine based on what we each learned on our individual journeys and how we learned to cope, and you can see the mass complexities of trying to unravel this mystery!

Growing up, I considered myself to be "in the world, but not of it," and knew I was a bit different than everyone around me. I was a truth seeker who did not accept the placated answers of society or those close to me, and had no desire to brush any tensions in my relationships that were entirely real to me under the rug. I would be the first to point out the elephant in the room, and though very social, I would be happier with no one around me than to live in relationships that were not authentic, transparent, or deeply intimate. I was often called "too sensitive," and told that I expected too much of people. What I've always known to be the truth, however, is that I could always see the potential in everyone and everything that they were either not able to see for themselves, or maybe were too afraid to look at. In times when it was fear holding them back, I could definitely understand their hesitation. Looking at the truth just might involve bucking the system to some degree, whether that be a larger societal system, or even just the partnership or family structure. We humans are social creatures, so to be ostracized, outcast, or punished for daring to dig further into what we could possibly become is very painful. The isolation, criticism, and belittling can be devastating, and therefore, many still live in fear and much potential is suppressed.

But Galileo knew his theories held relevance, and so did Einstein, Tesla, Gandhi, Martin Luther King, and Rosa Parks. No amount of mockery could sooth the restlessness in their souls that longed for the oneness, peace, harmony, and deep relationships we once experienced in spirit form. These people knew that heaven on earth was possible. They were not willing to silence themselves and fit in for the sake of acceptance and a quiet life of resignation. They could not.

They knew better, and they wanted more.

I could always see from the outside that to dig up and heal the damage done by eons of suppressive attempts to control the human psyche and keep us locked in a world of duality could free up the inner spark in all of us. Being able to personally touch the divine as we understood it and reconcile all that we were taught that brought us closer to conflict and competition, separateness and wrongness, would allow us to connect on the level where we know that we are all made of the same star dust.

If we can come to celebrate our own as well as each other's uniqueness, we can all give the gifts that are ours to give, and the world will function much better than it does when we are stifling ourselves or suppressing others, missing out on the rich talents that we could all benefit from.

Co-creation is only possible in oneness, therefore we will ultimately have to cooperate rather than compete in order to heal the earth and ourselves. This is why it is of the utmost importance to first heal the masculine and feminine within ourselves, then in our relationships, our families, our communities, our world, and our universe. If we attempt to co-create without this oneness and try to build on a wounded "separateness" consciousness, anything we build will not stand. It is time to put aside the notion that to "get ahead" means we must compete with each other at any cost, or that it's only possible for some of us to "win." This is just not the truth. When we co-create in beautiful harmony, so many bigger and more beautiful things can be accomplished, and everyone can feel like they got a fair shake. When everyone feels honored and respected, they will be less likely to experience the hopelessness that could cause them to inflict harm on themselves or others. We all want to belong, and we all want to feel honored and respected. Re-framing the old and worn out paradigm of competition over cooperation can breathe additional life into our dreams, goals, and desires. When we can support each other in our endeavors, eventually we all win.

Part One

Balance in All Things

Abraham Lincoln said, "A house divided against itself cannot stand." This is why peace, love, and oneness have not yet become fully grounded on our planet. The world of duality wants to stay in duality and has focused on that, thus creating the illusion of division inside of us and among us, coupled with the need to "do" something about it as an overly masculine response. In order to unite the two sides inside and out, we need to first tune into our feminine sides as we listen, connect, and BE with ourselves and each other as our full selves, every moment, in all of our vulnerability.

The ultimate divine marriage is that of the polarities; in this case both the inner and the outer marriage of the divine masculine and the divine feminine. Our patriarchal society has failed to achieve heaven on earth because of the mass suppression of feminine ideals such as: relating, gestating, and most of all creating a sacred container of "allowing" for things to emerge (See *Holding Space- A Guide to Supporting Others While Remembering to Take Care of Yourself First,* by this author). These things must be attended to first. Once these things are in place, then the masculine comes in and carries the ideas forth. The masculine (groups, classes, plans, structures) are what give the ideas born in the feminine container of resonance form, and the masculine is exactly the kind of physical matter, forward motion action that is needed to get them off the ground and bring them into reality. Every moment in history where the masculine (technology, progress, innovation, Western medicine) has been given preference over the feminine (indigenous ideals, nature, relationships, connection, holistic therapies), we have lost another piece of the puzzle. In order to reclaim it, we must uncover the ideals and ideas that have been marginalized by society as we progressed technologically, but sorely out of alignment with ourselves and our world.

One morning some years ago, I attended a Native American storytelling and music offering at my local library. The one thing that really stood out to me as I looked around the room was the wide diversity of very interested people that showed up. There were black people, white people, Asian people, Indian people, older people, and younger people. It seemed all of us were searching for something we'd lost.

In our overwhelmingly white and still masculine energy (science, logic, physicality) dominated Western world, it has become very evident that whether those of us that are searching realize what we are looking for or not, there is definitely something missing that we once had. It seems to me that the best places to go looking are the areas that have been ridiculed, rejected, and suppressed by our culture. Every trait or affiliation that has not been *allowed* by our society has been rejected due to the fear that people would be harder to control if they loved and approved of themselves or each other. The fear is that they would realize the truth of their connectedness—and no longer live in fabricated or exaggerated fear of things or others which "they are not." If these traits weren't repressed, people would then have the potential to realize what they've lost, to regain some of their wholeness, and to know that they are indeed a valuable part of the web of all life. They would know that the truth is that there is no separation—that we are ALL connected. The real truth is that there is no "us" and "them." In fact, it is quite possible that the suppressed and ostracized people and portions of society just might be the ones with the keys to save us all if we learn to follow their lead.

For those members of society that have been told that they are not "acceptable" for any reason, the healing journey for all of us can begin with you. Take a look at the parts of you (shadow-self) that have been deemed unacceptable by society and see if there is any good reason for pushing those parts of yourself away, or if in fact you've been lied to based on someone else's fear. The out of balance patriarchy has not just wounded the groups of people it has marginalized, it has wounded those who have long supported dominance of the masculine over the feminine rather than cooperation of the two energies as well. If you are a white male, it is time to reclaim all that has been taken from you as well. You were sold a lie, and you may have bought it. You were told that to claim the feminine energy in yourself would make you less of a man. The truth is, the Western world cannot survive on only masculine energy. Men cannot survive on only masculine energy within themselves. The task now for the males is to see past the lie and reclaim the other side of themselves, and to honor all of the people and places in the world and in themselves where that softer, feminine energy shows up.

The Dalai Lama has been quoted in recent years to have said "The world will be saved by the Western woman." I believe this is because the Western woman (representing and embodying the feminine) is completely fed up with being suppressed, and by circumstance in general has more means and time available than those in other cultures to devote to the personal growth work and advocacy that is needed to bring balance to all.

When we elevate and support those working heavily in the feminine (indigenous tribes, healers, artists, storytellers, etc.), we will all find our missing piece. But these keepers of the feminine cannot do it by themselves. Likewise, those working heavily the in the masculine (Western society, corporations, groups, structures, curricula) cannot complete this sacred marriage by themselves. We must shed the skin of the worn out and sorely out of balance patriarchy and realize that we need the feminine in order to co-create in resonance and bring forth those things that are truly longing to become manifest. I believe we are at a point in our civilization where we can no longer stand by while things continue to unravel. Courageous souls are beginning to come out en mass, rather than one by one. With the invention of the internet, we are more connected and better able to support each other in our goals and desires for a healthy, thriving society that works for all. The see-ers have been holding the space for this moment for eons, and are waiting to be called upon and compensated for their knowledge. We need them. They need us. The masculine and feminine, east and west, day and night, and sun and moon need each other to complete the balance. Just like we as humans need to be balanced in mind, body, and spirit in order to be healthy and thriving, so does our world. In a world of duality, it is imperative that the polarities be close to even in order to bring peace and harmony to all its inhabitants.

Atlantis and Lemuria

Whatever side of the coin you find yourself on in the "were Atlantis and Lemuria real?" debate, the stories of the mystical civilizations point to a similar point in history, when the reverence and honor for technology and power were becoming greater than (and not in balance with) the reverence and honor for nature, each other, and the desire to live in balance with all that exists. For the sake of brevity and to dissuade polarized discussion on whether or not they exist, I will leave it to you to decide if you'd like to delve further into this example, or at least this metaphor of the demise of an out-of-balance divine masculine and feminine civilization.

The Yin/Yang as a Symbol of the Balance of the Masculine and Feminine

In Eastern culture, we can examine the symbol of the yin/yang as an indicator of the importance as well as the inevitability of balance between and infusion of the masculine within the feminine and vice versa. In a definition taken directly from the online version of New World Encyclopedia: "Yin, the darker element, is passive, dark, feminine, downward-seeking, and corresponds to the night; yang, the brighter element, is active, light, masculine, upward-seeking and corresponds to the day. Yin and yang can be used to describe seasonal changes and directions, and can also be seen as a process of transformation. The concept probably originated to ancient agrarian religion; it exists in Confucianism, and it is prominent in Daoism. In traditional Chinese medicine, the "yang" organs meridian has a downward flow of energy (ch'i) and the "yin" organs meridian has an upward flow. An imbalance of the yin-yang ratio can cause illness... yin and yang are complementary, interdependent opposites, neither of which can exist without the other. Each can transform into the other, and contains a seed of the other within it. Yin and yang consume and support each other. Each aspect of yin and yang can be further subdivided into yin and yang aspects."

As you can see, even the academic definition is a deep dive down the rabbit hole of the need to blend and harmonize the masculine and feminine in every aspect of our lives. Of great interest to me in this definition is the fact that the yin/yang symbolizes an inter-dependence rather than dependence or independence. It seems society has adopted the idea (yet another polarity) that there are only the latter two. Somehow, to our great detriment, we missed the grey area of 'inter' dependence as an option "C," and simply, that one cannot exist without the other.

The "Two Spirits" In Pre-Contact Native America

In pre-contact Native America, gender was not something that was focused on, and that meant that someone's physiological makeup or tendency toward one gender or another was neither honored, nor feared. Though many members of the tribe identified with certain roles traditionally held by physiologically gendered males or females, there also existed genderless beings known as the Two Spirits, who were honored with holding a special place in the tribe. These Two Spirits expressed their masculine and feminine traits in whatever way felt suitable to them, and held roles such as healer, warrior, crafter, hunter, and chief. Instead of being shunned and outcast, as happened after colonization, these people were revered and honored for their uniqueness. The tribe knew that these people held a special gift to see the world from a unique perspective and honored them as such. As with many other native tribes that were stripped of their traditions and beliefs and forced to conform to Western society, many of these souls have slowly died a spiritual death due to suppression of their true nature, and lack of respect for the gifts they bring to the world.

Examples where the Masculine and Feminine Need to Synergize to Complete, Rather than Compete

Day/Night

What kind of life would any living thing have if it were never allowed to rest and restore itself? That is, what if there was an imbalance of day and night, or sun and moon? Though some may prefer one over the other, it defies argument that one is better than the other. All living things need daylight and sun in order to grow and regenerate. We also need a balance of the two opposites so that we can allow ourselves to rest during one phase, and work and play during the other. The day (in general), represents the masculine energies of action and doing, whereas the night represents the feminine energies of rest, dreaming, and restoration of resources. We can look at growing food as an example. If it were daytime all of the time, crops would burn up rather than have the right amount of sun in which to flourish. This would surely affect life on earth.

Western/Eastern Medicine

We can also look for a moment at Western (masculine) and Eastern (feminine) medicine. As mentioned before, though Western medicine is superior when it comes to broken bones or other instant trauma to body parts, we have seen its inferiority to Eastern medicine and holistic therapies when it comes to chronic illnesses or other diseases, mental or physical. In order to give ourselves the best medical system, the two belief systems will need to harmonize and synergize, offering a complete and holistic look at human health. There is much to be said here as well for the prevention aspect that Eastern or holistic medicine considers. If we allow the two systems to work together, we may have less need for the billions of dollars spent on Western therapies that either don't work or compound symptoms, as many diseases and disorders will never have the chance to take root or escalate.

Western/Indigenous Culture

In order to achieve optimal emotional health as individuals and society, bringing together Western (masculine) and Indigenous (feminine) cultures could pay massive dividends toward the peace and harmony we seek individually and collectively. It is wrong to think that one culture is superior to the other. Just think about the options available for food and entertainment in your town for an easy example. Do you go to the same type of movie and eat the same type of food every day? If not, chances are you see the benefit in being well-rounded in your entertainment and culinary choices. In fact, most people refer to that type of well-roundedness as being "cultured." The very phrase points to the fact that to experience different entertainment and food is to experience different cultures. If we understand and accept this as part of our experience in our daily food and entertainment choices, it should make sense that to integrate ideals from different cultures into our being would make us more well-rounded as individuals as well.

If we take the Western ideals of industrial and technological progress and couple them with the Indigenous ideals of our connectedness with the earth and all of life, we will make more decisions that are sustainable and life-giving, rather than to barrel full speed ahead into progress and technology without considering the aspects of a healthy mind, body, soul, and planet. How will we enjoy the progress if we feel dead inside? It seems to me that most people choose to vacation in beautiful areas, alive with nature. Therefore one can assume that it would truly be a tragedy that if we continue to work so hard on industrial progress without considering indigenous wisdoms of connectedness with all of life, we won't have any more beautiful places to vacation to.

Physical and Non-Physical (Science and Spirituality)

To balance our physical and non-physical worlds we will need to reconcile the split we have between things such as: sexuality and spirituality; balancing the new paradigm we are working towards with the old paradigm that still exists in our physical world; and basically all that we can sense through our five senses with all that we cannot that has already been explored in the areas of: quantum and meta physics, energy medicine (including chakras), earth's energy, the Schumann resonance, etc. Living in human designed systems based on control and fear, we have failed to harmonize these elements, or even recognize that they exist in some cases. This has caused the shadow aspect of many of these areas to rear its head, resulting in things like: disease, sexual misconduct, subtle mind control, and quite often just feeling completely out of alignment with the world that we live in.

Some examples of this imbalance and therefore shadow effect include strict religious policies that forbid healthy sexual expression. The suppression of the sexual/creative energy with no guidance on where to channel it in healthy physical ways has caused both clergy and parishioners to act out sexually in ways that are dangerous, harmful, or inappropriate to themselves and others. Had they been allowed to balance their spiritual sides with their physical sides, and taught about the energy of the second chakra (the seat of sexuality AND creative energy), they may have been able to harmonize with themselves and the shadow side would not have come out in such a dangerous way.

It is when we cut off one side of ourselves or our world that the imbalance can result in disease, violence, mistreatment, or unhealthy behaviors. We absolutely need to balance our spiritual sides with our physical sides in order to lead a godly life in our earthly bodies. We were given all of the beautiful and wonderful physical pleasures to enjoy, but also the free will to experience them in both healthy and unhealthy ways. I believe that arming people with the information they need to make healthy decisions and to accept themselves for the spiritual and physical beings that they are will reduce the shame, blame, and anger that many bury that in turn comes out in less than desirable ways.

Sex and Love (Listed Intentionally in That Order to Illustrate the Imbalance)

Sex

Why do modern humans seem so intrigued with sex? In a heavily masculine energy dominated world where we aren't encouraged to look at our feelings and the only way we are told we can access the divine is through approved channels—sex can appear to be the only option for personally experiencing a connection to that which is greater than us. It is the physical manifestation of the masculine and feminine coming together in the divine (feminine) energy. Energetically, whether the partners are male and female or same-sex partners (note that in same-sex pairings, one partner will typically embody more of the opposite gender's energy), when entered with reverence and respect, the energy of the divine masculine and feminine come together in perfect union in this state.

When so many other aspects of our lives are governed by systems that claim to know what's best for each of us individually, sex is the only way some people will allow themselves to touch the divine. Sex (when accessed with love) is one of the only channels to the divine in which no mainstream authority claims to educate us on what the correct way is to experience it (unless it's to stay away from it entirely). It is left up to each individual to trust that they have the key to access this channel to the divine on their own, and that whatever their experience is or that they would like it to be (again, when entered into in a healthy manner), is the right one for them.

Unhealthy expressions of sex can occur when a person gets too heavily indoctrinated into a masculine dominated world. They become caught in the rhythm of doing at the expense of being, as well as starved for the connection to the other side of themselves and the world. If a person is starving, the sensation may lead them to try to take by force what will not end up working out in their favor energetically. When people overpower others sexually, they are trying to use control and force (divine masculine energies in their unhealthy form) in an attempt to access the divine feminine side in themselves that they are disconnected from. In this example, the starving person is trying to feed off of another's spiritual energy in a way that will never satiate them. The result is energetic trauma to the person they're attempting to overpower without gaining what it is they're after anyway—a no-win situation for both parties as well as the world at large due to the negative energy expelled during the trauma and thereafter. As depicted in any movie where the villain tries to gain "power" by physically overpowering an individual or group of people, the end result always teaches that you cannot steal divine power—it must be cultivated and accessed from within.

Of course we know that anything in excess is not good for balance in an individual or a system (try eating chocolate cake for breakfast every day). Although sex can be an enjoyable and wonderful way to cultivate this spiritual energy, we must also remember that there are going to be many times in life when sex is not desired, not possible, not what's best, or not appropriate. Even if we are partnered, there will be times when we will need to grow individually and blending our spiritual and physical energies by engaging in sex may not be what's best for our spiritual or emotional ascension.

Thank goodness we have been given many other ways of accessing the divine feminine! We can experience nature, do something creative, meditate, treat ourselves in a sensual manner (sensuality does not always co-exist with sexuality—in fact they can be very separate), do our inner work, experience something beautiful, or any number of other ideas. By using other methods to experience the divine (feminine) energy throughout our lives, we can be sure that we are spiritually fed and are balancing our masculine sides with our feminine sides, and that sex is by no means our only option of experiencing this union. When a larger percentage of us choose this in our own lives, the scales will tip, and the outer world will begin to reflect the inner world that will reside in the majority of us.

Love

Love is something we all want, and it is inherently feminine in nature. We allow ourselves to seek, feel, and know love—and yet we can't quantify it. This is proof that although our world is sorely out of balance toward the masculine energy right now, there is still a strong force of the feminine that is inherently latent in all of us, no matter what our situation in life. There is hope to change the world we see on the news every day, and it exists within each one of us.

Love is the highest, non-physical state we can achieve. It is the epitome of divine feminine energy. What most of us haven't been told by society, however, is that the key to augmenting this state of being in our lives and our world begins within ourselves. In order to truly attain the peace we seek as souls in physical embodiment, we must begin by loving ourselves. When we start there, we are better able to love others and accept their love in return. We also become better equipped to receive the things that are good for us and nurture our minds, bodies, and souls. When we learn to access love within ourselves on a daily basis, we open the channel in ourselves to receive divine ideas, beauty, joy, and love in the feminine energy that we can bring forth into all of our earthly expressions.

How do we channel love? We speak kindly to ourselves in our heads and with our words. We remember our successes over our perceived failures. We re-frame our failures and see them instead as the lessons that we received, or the ways in which we grew and moved forward after experiencing them. We allow ourselves to exist in a world which may not have reached the critical tipping point yet, holding the knowing that it will if each one of us can channel that love within ourselves. We look for the good or the lesson in everything—being sure to also notice the times when we are being shown that we must strengthen ourselves and respond to that which is not healthy for us or our world. We learn to rise above our challenges and face them from a higher perspective, understanding the greater picture unfolding. We surround ourselves with kind and loving people and animals, and remember to tap in to things that put us back in this vibration (nature, books, movies, music, life coaching, friends, things we enjoy in a healthy manner). We live in gratitude and reverence for ourselves and all life, and we become one with all that exists in the universe.

Part Two

Why the Feminine Must Go First

This is quite possibly the most important section in this entire book. I am not kidding when I say that.

Now before any of the men reading start cultivating the inner fuel necessary to either put the book down or throw it across the room, bear with me a minute. If you are still feeling triggered, ask yourself if you have any interest in multiple days of painful cramping as well as a menstrual cycle for around a week every, single, month. If you've settled down a bit and decided to stay with me after that, I give you my complete respect—as you are willing to open up to one of the biggest truths that has never been widely shared.

The feminine must go first. That doesn't necessarily always mean that the women must go first, but then again, sometimes it does. Again, please stay with me as I attempt to make this crystal clear. Let's start with art and creativity, just to make it easier.

In order to produce great art, whether it be writing, music, visual art, dance, storytelling, or anything else, the creator must allow themselves to open up to the greater universal field of creativity. This is a feminine energy. If the creator attempts to jump with their mind (masculine) to the masculine side of art (getting it ready for public consumption, marketing, etc.), it is most likely that their creation will not be very fantastic. If an artist does not allow themselves to surrender to the creative field, they are denying themselves the access to all that would give their creation the rich content and depth that is possible for it. Even if the creation is meant solely to be colorful, entertaining, or beautiful, with no deeper meaning, it will shine that much brighter if the artist allows themselves that surrender. Art is meant to touch the soul, be beautiful, or inspire contemplation. How can it do that if it were created only in the masculine energy of "thinking" about how it can be packaged, marketed, and consumed by the person experiencing it?

Other examples of the feminine needing to go first can be seen in business, technology, and progress, all very masculine concepts. As we have been able to clearly see in recent years, when businesses operate either solely in the masculine, or from the masculine before the feminine, they have not considered their impact on the earth and its people and are often completely unsustainable, and even dangerous to the continuation of life on the planet. When a business is started from masculine energy and operates solely in masculine energy, it is suppressing the feminine in its infrastructure, as well as the ripple effects it will have on everything that it touches. Businesses that operate in this way can destroy the earth and its inhabitants, cause depressed, controlled and unhealthy employees, and a host of other maladies. The only people this type of business seems to benefit are the ones at the top, making the profits. Here's the bad news though, it actually doesn't benefit them either, as they have to "sell their soul to the devil" by trading in basic humanity and spirituality for profits, leading them to be sorely out of balance with their own inner feminine sides.

Spirituality (I will not discuss religion here as it is spirituality taken into its masculine form, which must be done with a balanced consideration for a healthy physical life in harmony with a healthy spiritual life or it can be quite damaging for people as well) is another example of where the feminine must go first. Since I am looking at it as universal spirituality without regard to any particular belief system, let's look at a person's individual relationship with whatever they consider to be greater than them and their physical world, and nature.

God/Universe/Creator/Love/The Quantum Field (whatever word you like here), operates of its own accord and may very well be in direct opposition from that which we believe we'd like to experience on a day to day basis. It exists that way in order to teach, provide opportunities to grow and get stronger, or bring pieces and people together in order to choose the life we wish to create, as much as we are allowed to do so with our earthly power of will. Nature exists in much the same way. "Mother" feminine nature can bring us beautiful sunny days filled with warm breezes and fragrant flowers, or it can howl with tornadoes, storms, floods, earthquakes, and tsunamis. Though some of our human actions can affect the outcome of the natural world, in many cases it operates completely independent of our will or desires. We cannot tame Mother Nature, nor should we try to.

What we must understand is that there is something far greater than us that we are a part of, and that though we control much of our individual world with our will, we certainly do not control all of it. In order to work within a world that we cannot fully control, we must be willing to surrender to the feminine (that which is greater than us, nature, etc.) in order to truly co-create with the universe that we are a part of, and give ourselves a better chance of feeling peaceful, balanced, and in the flow of life.

If you have tried to create something in your life over and over again by sheer will alone, perhaps it's time to surrender to the feminine. Stop trying to solve the issue in the energy it was created in (Einstein) and try handing it over to a higher energy in order to solve it on a higher level and begin to move the pieces around in the physical world in order for it to manifest into physical reality. (Feel free to look to prayer, the Law of Attraction, or any aspect of quantum physics, metaphysics, etc. for help with this).

A personal example of this actually occurred during the writing of this book.

For months, I had been getting the divine guidance to work on writing this book. I had already surrendered to my higher power (so I thought) by pretty much asking for guidance on just about everything I need to make a decision on, every day (I did have to work previously for a few years on how to distinguish what was my ego self in my head and what was my higher guidance, and even then, which beings were benevolent and which were not), but this was taking it even further. I had been worried about bills and how to pay them for the last few months. I had been guided to quit my part-time job and look for another one that was work-at-home, flexible, and less than 20 hours per week to supplement my other endeavors. I hadn't found that yet though, and our income was much less than what we needed to pay out. Also during this time, we had extra expenses pop up that we had to take care of. Being an overly responsible person most of my life, I tried to "solve" the problem by getting side jobs here and there to make up for the lack of money, because that's what you should do, right? Well, after a while, that didn't work anymore. One thing after another began to fail—seminars I planned would only get two participants, people would cancel on jobs they had booked me for, and other messages from the great beyond that my "will" wasn't going to cut it anymore. I had higher stress and anxiety, and no results. I was too worried about solving my problem to spend much time with the book, and in the end, I found I had neither written very much, nor solved my income issue. So I surrendered, again, even harder this time than I thought I already had. And then I was led to a book that began to change my world. Interestingly enough, the only reason I obtained this book was because I had to purchase one of my own books for a seminar participant that I chose to do through Amazon because it would be faster, and then decided I should get another book for myself to qualify for free shipping. In reading this book and doing the exercises, I began to uncover even deeper blocks I had been carrying around, learned that there was even more space for me to surrender to my higher power in, and also that I had still been trying to control and fix things in the same energy they were created in (very masculine "action" steps rather than surrendering to the "feminine").

It begs to be shared here that much of our (male or female) resistance to surrendering to that which is greater than us comes from the fear we experience in our physical world. Fear that we either learned or absorbed through others or our own experiences throughout our lifetime. Fear that can only be overcome by surrendering (and then working in cooperation with) something that is above that fear, to help heal it and grant us infinitely more energy to create in by clearing it from our systems. In order to bring to fruition what we truly desire and know to be good and healthy to ourselves and all of those around us, we must be willing to surrender some of our will to something higher than us that can orchestrate the pieces in a way we never could have imagined.

Now this section would be incomplete if I did not at least touch on the fact that as females, we are physiologically more in tune with the feminine, and therefore also much more innately intuitive. Though I am not suggesting that any man bow to or acquiesce solely to the whims of a woman, when there is one in your life who is deeply engaged in her personal work, surrendering to what is greater than her, and following a path of honesty and integrity no matter what the consequences, you may want to pay attention to what she is guiding you towards even if the physical evidence does not seem to support it. Again, you will definitely want to go to your own inner feminine (higher power, intuition, etc.) and be sure you understand it well enough to know that it is in fact your higher benevolent guidance that you are listening to before you make any decisions. I'm just letting you know that the woman who has done a giant chunk of that work on herself and is naturally more intuitive, may be on to something that is more sustainable and ultimately more nurturing to all those involved.

In relation to this section, Sam Keen's, *Fire in the Belly- On Being a Man,* may also be of interest to you. This book began my journey down the rabbit hole of healing the masculine and feminine many years ago, though I had no idea of it back then.

** For those of you who were offended at the beginning of this section but are still reading... first, I thank you. You are obviously willing to listen to my argument. But if you still want to throw the book across the room, I humbly ask you to consider just one more thing. The concept of using the feminine energy before the masculine energy is nothing personal. Here's a great example I like to use—imagine you are having a house built and are hiring all of your own contractors. Before any work is started, the electrician comes to you and makes a case that they should be allowed to work on the house first, before any of the other contractors. As you can see, there would be nothing personal against the electrician as you try to explain that you honor and respect them and their contributions, but that it just isn't possible to put wiring in place before the walls exist. Nothing personal against the electrician, it's just the way things need to be done for maximum results.

How Honoring/Entering Into Feminine Energy First, Followed by Masculine Energy
Will Pay Dividends Individually and Collectively

Relationships with Ourselves, That Which is Greater Than Us, and Others

The first and most significant area where entering into and honoring the feminine energy first will pay dividends is in our relationships. Relationships are feminine in energy, so if we've learned to function solely by our masculine energy (as most of us in Western society were taught in school and by the many messages of society), we're going to have real trouble in that area. This is so very sad, as relationships are the things that most of us really live for. Every study asking people on their deathbeds what they wish they would have done more of in their lives reveals people's regret with experiences or relationships—not that they wished that they would have "worked more," found better ways to make more money, marketed to more people, or got further ahead financially. The truth about money is that it is something our society invented as a means of energy exchange when we provide a product or service for someone else. Money is a masculine energy. Even if our work is in the feminine (counseling, teaching, etc.), most often the way we reach our clients or students is through the masculine energy (marketing, school, corporations, etc), and the means of being compensated for that work is through the masculine system of money. So if we only focus on all the means of making money, and not on the relationship/experience side of things, we miss opening ourselves up to the reason we put all of that work into sustaining our physical existence in the first place.

What good is it to be able to afford the nicest things if we don't know how to enjoy ourselves or our time with others when we experience them? Most people work in order to provide sustenance and pleasure to their lives. Since our most important relationships are with our higher power and ourselves—even if we prefer to do everything alone, it seems to me that being able to enjoy the feminine energy of relationship is at the top of everyone's list—and therefore considering the feminine energy aspects to enjoying your life is worth giving priority to.

There are many areas within relationships where entering into the feminine energy first will pay dividends as well. Within our relationships (even the ones with ourselves), we need to make decisions, solve problems, and negotiate (feminine qualities) in order to move anything forward (masculine quality). So getting to know ourselves well by spending time journaling, contemplating, working with our higher power, meditating, working with a counselor/coach, and reading books is a worthwhile expenditure of our time and energy. When we know ourselves well, we can present ourselves in authentic and honest ways to others, and learn to honor both sides as we make decisions, negotiate, and move forward with our plans, dreams, and actions (masculine energies). Spending the time in the feminine first will allow these decisions to be made with greater harmony and ease, and will allow the masculine (action) steps to unfold beautifully.

Manifesting Our Dreams

Have you ever tried to manifest something, even perhaps "worked really hard" on it, but it just never materialized? Without getting too heavily into quantum physics, psychology, or spirituality here, I can say that one of three things may have happened. First, the thing you wished for perhaps wasn't in your best interest, and you were saved by the universe/divine by the fact that it did not manifest for you. Second, that though you put all of the action energy into it, you were missing the feminine energy that may not have been lined up with what you said you desired. In order to manifest anything, we cannot be in direct resistance to it. Though we may think we are clear and ready to go, many of us have subconscious blocks and old tapes running through our heads that teach us to fear that which we seek, tell us we are not good enough, etc. These things can only be accessed through the feminine energy. The interesting thing to note here is that this phenomenon has actually been studied and proven by science (masculine), spirituality (feminine), as well as quantum physics and metaphysics (combinations of science and spirituality). The fact is that every one of these traditions has proven that if you don't clear what is blocking your subconscious, no amount of labor, time, and physical effort will allow your creation to sprout, and if it does, it may not be sustainable. Third, it may have been a very big goal and there were a lot of pieces that needed to line up in order for it to manifest fully and in all of its grandness, and perhaps you gave up too soon.

A Sustainable Planet to Play, Work, and Live On

In order to enjoy relationships and have the ability to manifest our dreams into physical reality, we need a planet to live, work, and play on. This is why the third area where entering into feminine energy first will pay dividends is sustainable, environmentally friendly people, companies, and leadership who consider the next seven generations in all of their decisions. The "Seventh Generation" principle is at the heart of most Native American traditions, and was included as a major portion of the Great Law of Peace of the Iroquois. The law states that before embarking on any new idea, project, product, service, etc., that a person or group consider the effect their decision might have on the next seven generations of people, plants, animals, water, etc.; in essence, everything that is essential to all life and enjoyment of the planet. By going back to these old teachings (which I found through research that the U.S. Constitution was actually based on, but left out major aspects of—including the Seventh Generation rule and the way women were to be treated in community leadership positions), and giving precedence to the feminine energies of right relationship with ourselves and the earth before any undertaking, we can ensure that our creations are not only functional and beautiful, but sustainable too. In this way, we are allowing for continued living and thriving on this planet long after each one of us departs this earthly realm.

We have long seen the disastrous effects of ignoring the feminine in favor of "controlling" mother nature in any way possible, even those ways in which we have no business meddling. Living in harmony with nature and therefore the feminine, as well as extending the chivalry to pay attention to her needs ahead of our physical creations is not only a good thing to, but will ultimately benefit each and every one of us, even those who still choose not to think about it.

Unraveling the Difference Between the Divine Masculine and Feminine as Energies and Men and Women as People

A very important distinction, and one where many of us can get stuck in life, can happen when our subconscious unwittingly combines the concept of masculine and feminine energies with people who show up as males and females.

Let's start with an example. Say you are a male, and identify as a male. When you were growing up, your mother was severely abusive. Though she was only one female, and you may learn throughout your life not to project that persona onto other females you come across, there is another possible snag that can occur. It is possible that in trying to shield yourself from the emotional pain that came from your mother, you decided that feelings, emotions, and relationships themselves were scary. In order to not feel the pain your mother caused, you decided it was dangerous to get close to anyone, or to feel much of anything at all. In effect, you unknowingly buffered yourself from the divine feminine within yourself. This can cause all sorts of issues, both emotional and physical, and can show up in your life by blocking you from potential jobs, relationships, and opportunities that may require you to allow yourself to explore the inner workings of your psyche before they become manifest.

On the other side, say you are a woman and you grew up with an abusive father. As the world of work and money are masculine energies, if you have not learned to separate the fact that your father who was a male and caused you pain from the divine masculine energies of work, business, and money, you may experience much trouble in these areas. In this case, you could grow up with the desire and talent to follow a certain career path, but continually be derailed because the part of you that remembers your father as abusive somehow lumped that together with divine masculine energies. In your desire to keep yourself safe from harm, you are unable to take the action steps in the masculine that are needed to move forward, and your career never quite takes off.

In these cases, what has happened is that your subconscious blurred the female or male figure that caused you physical or emotional trauma with the divine feminine and masculine energies that govern emotions/relationships and vocation. It will take some work to unravel the feminine or masculine energies from the male or female who caused you pain, and to begin to access those sides of your inner landscape, enabling you to function as a whole and healthy being in the world. The quest is to realize that although it was a woman or man who hurt you, it was only the specific physiologically embodied male or female that caused you pain, not the divine masculine or feminine energies themselves.

Part Three

The Individual, Intimate Partnerships, Families, and Greater Society
"How the Microcosm Affects the Macrocosm"

Healing on an Individual Level (Self-Healing)

In order to heal the world, we must heal ourselves first. Investigating the root of our beliefs, wounds, and pain is a process that many hesitate to undertake. It involves vulnerability, and a surrendering of control. It involves a giant leap into the great unknown, courage to face the truths as well as the untruths, and trusting what we do not know, allowing it to guide and heal us. To heal ourselves is to continually be with and meet those challenges head on one by one, as we come through to the other side a little more each time. This level of healing is at the core of healing for all relationships. To heal the masculine and feminine on any level, we must start at the individual level. The individual must find where they are out of balance, where the wounding to the inner as well as embodied (whether we are male or female) masculine and feminine exists, and apply grace, further discovery, wisdom, healing, and forgiveness in order to pave the way for healing on a grander scale of the masculine and feminine within us ALL. This requires great courage and surrender and is not for the faint of heart, yet lies at the very core of beginning to build an equalitarian society full of co-creators who stand side by side with each other in experiencing all of the gifts life has to offer.

In embarking on the self-healing journey through surrender and commitment to discovering the truth, greater self-love and reverence for all things will spring forth. There is much wisdom to be found in our shadows and foibles. When we stop reaching for perfection, or perhaps agnosticism or indifference, we will begin to regain our balance as humans—sacred containers for both the divine and the physical, and yet another polarity to be balanced. There are many untruths to be faced as we go through our inner worlds and sort through what is truly ours, and what we have unintentionally taken on as ours through our experiences in society and with others. Every time a person has the courage to do the tough inner work required to dig up their false and limiting beliefs, they undoubtedly affect those around them. Even if those around them kick and scream and resist the person's changes, it is impossible to remain unaffected by one passionate enough to dare to be their full and complete self. Examining what we know to be our own imbalances in our masculine and feminine aspects is the key to understanding others and beginning to balance our world. What were we told as children about how we are to act as embodied males or females? How much of this is true? How much is based on cultural norms and outdated memes that may no longer apply, and may never have applied to true oneness?

In order for both men and women to heal and break free of an imbalanced patriarchal system that works for neither of them, both genders must return to self-love and self-healing and refrain from supporting that system by continuing to blindly follow its regime. We live in a world that has encouraged us not to know ourselves. It has encouraged us to give our power away, numb ourselves, and otherwise run from the inner reflection that would make true cooperation, great relationships, and a more peaceful world a stronger reality. We must begin the dive into who we are and what makes us tick in order to understand how to show up more authentically in the world, and to consciously build a life that is in alignment with our truth. When we do this, we begin to attract people and experiences that help us to become the brightest versions of ourselves, leaving us feeling free and full of excitement and possibility.

The Men

Let's first speak of the men. In the Western world, it seems that any balanced sense of the healthy inner masculine has become so far from a man's experience in recent history that it has almost been entirely squeezed out. Western culture as well as other patriarchies have conditioned men to believe that true masculine power lies in control and domination, which is really just the out of balance form of divine masculine energy—and is not where true divine power is accessed. Men have not been culturally supported in accessing their feminine sides, mostly due to lack of understanding by society of what masculine and feminine energies really are. To access your "feminine side" as a male or your "masculine side" as a female doesn't make you any less your gender physiologically. It has all been a misuse and misunderstanding of what the words masculine and feminine really mean in all of their depth and complexity. Attending self-help groups, talking about feelings, and basically any action that would put a man in touch with the other half of himself are still largely unapproved by society. In a culture where men are told to "man up," and that "boys don't cry," men have had to continually shut down and forgo this window of access to the other part of themselves except in relationship with a woman.

In large part, men are so hungry for their other half; many have come to believe that their only access is to be found in the opposite sex, which is damaging to both sexes. In relationships between the two when the feminine side is shown to them through a woman, a man will often shut it down solely due to the foreignness of the feelings. When we deny a part of ourselves that needs expression, it often comes out in unhealthy ways. Throughout history, this has manifested in things such as suppression of women, violence, sexual abuse and assault, and believing that conquering a woman in any way defines their manhood. The truth is that the men are hurting. They're hurting so badly they don't even know it. They have been fed and bought the idea that they must compete as individuals to be successful, and that they must always be in control. As the out of balance patriarchal society that we live in encourages and supports the advancement of the individual rather than interconnectedness and cooperation for the benefit of all, it is no surprise that with this type of cultural conditioning, men as a whole have not been trained to easily understand the divine feminine principles of what it takes to be in relationship with either the self or other. Men yearn for the same mutually satisfying relationships women yearn for, the same brotherhoods that we as social creatures thrive on. They desire close relationships with other male friends, those who they know without a doubt have their backs. Unfortunately, it seems that one of the only places men in our society are culturally allowed to cultivate this brotherhood is through military service, built for the purposes of preparing for and participating in war with an enemy. The unfortunate truth in this case is that in many societies this "brotherhood" seeks to exterminate an enemy from the greater "brotherhood" of the human race through war. It seems men in our society have been taught that we must always have an "enemy" and watch our backs. Even sports, politics, and scientific discoveries have shifted from containers of healthy competition and places to discover grand ideas designed to benefit all, to races to be won against another person or group of people at any cost.

It is little wonder that within this construct of an out of balance masculine society based on power, control, and competition, that both the healthy masculine and feminine have been suppressed in men, women, and greater society itself. Many men are so far from their inner feminine that it will indeed take courage for both them and the women around them to step into their full power to own the divine feminine as well as the divine masculine in an equal and balanced way. It will take much introspection into who they really are, and a desire to uncover the truth of how an overly patriarchal society does not serve them any more than it under-serves the women. As women are closer to their divine feminine and are waking up to reclaiming it, men can greatly benefit as well at this time through allowing and supporting the women around them in coming into their true feminine, in turn supporting their return home to their true masculine.

Since the change in gender roles after the women's movement, old scripts playing in men's heads continue to stall them in their quest for understanding and thriving in a new paradigm. From an out of date patriarchy based on control, rigidity, fiercely providing, etc., men are attempting to shift from what has fallen, to the new world that has not yet emerged. Men are left teetering on the edge between shifting from master to mate in relationships, from provider to parent in the family, and from workhorse to actual enjoyment in their jobs in the workplace. In order to change the old paradigm still at play, men will have to be willing to encourage each other to embrace balance and harmony within themselves, with women, and within the world in the new paradigm. Western males have been sold a sorry package of what it means to be a man, much to their detriment. They have been promised a world of power, with no indication of the true inner power necessary to achieve self-power and therefore self-mastery. The package of superiority the Western men have been sold has many times given them nothing more than inner emptiness and often outer manifestations of failed relationships (because relationships are a feminine energy), careers that suck the life out of them, and sometimes even prison or addictions.

If we are to achieve heaven on earth, men will need to remember some of the "old ways" of husbandry for themselves, the land, their families, and their communities, while balancing the modern conveniences and comforts that years of patriarchy have brought as their gifts. The "old" mentors must return to bring them back what they have given away in exchange for technology, rather than having incorporated the two together. In our current lives of offices and artificial environments filled with competition rather than cooperation, there seem to be a lack of places where men can work as a team to fulfill a common goal toward the health and benefit of humanity. An environment such as this could serve as a place for a man to really come in to his manhood, but alas, these opportunities are scarce, and those that do exist are not looked upon with favor by the majority just yet.

In the meantime, perhaps one way men can begin the process of building a healthy masculine side as well as embracing their inner feminine is through learning to become as attentive to their roles of father and husband and/or growing and finding themselves spiritually or emotionally, as they are to their outside work. In this way, they could find the completeness of their manhood, and contribute to the "team" atmosphere required for a healthy, thriving intimate relationship and family (only if family life is what they choose of course). Unfortunately, instead of looking to this arena to channel their energy and complete their rite of passage, many men have become so accustomed to the competition energy they've been indoctrinated into that they end up competing with their partners as well, and as we've discovered in a previous chapter, a house divided against itself can't stand. How sad this has been for families, couples, and the children growing up in these families where the relationship does not ever harmonize, and the father many times either gives up completely or at the very least is separated from his children.

Of particular concern is the predicament that today's boys are in. They are still bombarded with outdated masculine roles through the media and those around them, in addition to many being raised in homes with no fathers. In a world where technology is heralded as the only worthwhile pursuit, this renewed focus on husbandry of all aspects of a man's life could bring them back to the meaningful work of 'husbanding' the next generations through attending to the family, community, or the earth, balanced with any additional outside income producing "work." Of course I am not insinuating that a man must marry and have a family in order to achieve this goal. Inner husbandry of the man's soul is always a path to completeness of the polarities. As mentioned before, women can help men regain this side of themselves, but they must be able to find it themselves first.

The Women

The essential work for women is to uncover and then step into their true divine feminine. This is at the root of healing for all humans, male and female, at this essential time in history—but since women also embody more of the feminine physiologically, it is that much closer for them to reach. Our world is no longer sustainable due to too many years of a patriarchy run rampant, and the majority of women in Western society are as sorely out of touch with their inner feminine as the men. This is grand work for the women. They must begin the task of uncovering and healing all that has been suppressed, shamed, and abused about their very feminine essence. They must uncover all of the same lies as the men were told about what it means to be man or woman. This is no easy feat. Even tougher is the fact that many unhealed men are competing with and separating from these women in droves. They do not understand what is taking place, the inner voice that is driving the women to reclaim their true selves, and they don't understand that their own ticket to healing just may be through supporting the women who are still close enough to their nurturing and intuitive natures to find this inner voice. This awakening, along with the fact that women have been culturally encouraged to accept and integrate their masculine sides since the women's movement, has caused deep changes in the structural foundation of what relationships have been for many years. In the Western world for the most part, gone are the days of marrying for convenience or survival. Today's couples are searching for conscious partnerships where there is internal growth and thriving, and the awakened women who are on the quest to recover their suppressed feminine are leading the charge.

Something else to notice here is that the feminine speaks in quiet, subtle ways. Perhaps the reason it has been hard to hear by females as well as larger society during an out of balance patriarchy, is that the masculine voice is loud and powerful, and the feminine, quiet and subtle. Consider the voice of God or Spirit—to truly know it and be able to surrender to its guidance, one must be able to hear it. Women thus far have had a bit of a rough time uncovering the feminine as it is so deeply buried, shamed, and shunned. They have also had a hard time uncovering their inner masculine as married to their inner feminine, as their voices as embodied women have been essentially silenced by a masculine run culture, which has in turn become the voice of their inner dominating masculine as well. Thankfully, true divine feminine work on a larger level has been done quietly and kept alive throughout the eons by many indigenous cultures. The sad fact is that colonial (patriarchal) cultures found no use for these feminine aspects of society and therefore missed the chance to join in co-creation with them. We are still working to get this back. The women of today must be willing to stand up and live their full truth, no longer hiding or silencing themselves due to outdated cultural imprints of what is appropriate behavior for a woman in society. However, they must also take on the monumental task of healing themselves, and freeing the men to do the same, in turn co-creating a more beautiful and sustainable family structure for our society to build on—for our culture still does not allow for men to begin to work on their inner wounds and to truly feel themselves without appearing "weak."

Healing on a Partnership Level (Healing in Marriages, Friendships, and Business Partnerships)

As discussed in the previous section, once we have achieved a good level of personal healing, our self-love will have grown, greatly affecting the quality of our relationships with others. Doing the inner work, and learning to love and honor ourselves and others will then allow for shadow work to be completed in safe and loving environments. In these containers, each party (after their individual healing) will become strong enough to hold witness to the other as they transform, while also possessing the necessary amount of detachment needed to be able to witness the other's pain without jumping in to "fix" anything. (Again, see *Holding Space- A Guide to Supporting Others While Remembering to Take Care of Yourself First,* by this author). Mastering how to create safe containers such as these will also allow each partner to show up as their whole and true selves, without the need to hide, mask, or conceal who they really are to placate the other. In order to do this to our maximum ability, we must be willing to look into our thought patterns, beliefs, and cultural norms, and look at how and why our relationships with others and our environment have become so unbalanced in the first place. (See end of book for exercises on how to create these strong containers within a relationship so people can show up authentically).

For centuries, we have been taught by our authority systems to "do unto others as we would have them do unto us." This is all well and good, but somewhere along the way that idea became unbalanced as well, and people started giving everything to others to please them, sacrificing their own truths along the way. If we sacrifice our own truth or authenticity, we suffer. If we sacrifice our own truth or authenticity, our relationships suffer. How can our relationships thrive if we are not showing up as we truly are, and relating to each other from that truth? How can our partnerships grow if we constantly stuff our truths down in order to do what we think the other would like, when most often what our partners really want is to know exactly who it is that they are in a relationship with, with complete transparency? For relationships to achieve true intimacy, we must trust both ourselves and our partners enough with the truth of who we really are. If we can meet ourselves as well as our partner or friend in that space, we have truly found a person we can be our authentic selves with. When we find ourselves in these truly intimate relationships, much growth is possible. When we allow ourselves to be vulnerable enough to share our true selves conversations can be had, beliefs can be challenged, hurts can be healed, and growth can be exponential.

Thus, allowing ourselves to heal individually while remaining authentic to ourselves will result in partnerships that will allow for deeper collaboration, more intimacy, and more satisfaction. Another product of these healthier unions can be healthier "children," whether human children, or creative or business projects that have sprung forth out of these partnerships. These healthier "children" will no doubt lead to stronger bonds and structures on the group level. Women and men coming together as "one" in their embodiments of the masculine and feminine either in marriage, intimate partnerships, or business partnerships can exponentially increase the creative potential for humanity. As these partners find union, they remain independent while also becoming interdependent. The creative power and force for good within the duo is exponentially more powerful than one when combined in graceful harmony and co-creation, rather than competition and separateness. Nature provides all sorts of examples of these types of cooperative, symbiotic relationships that increase the quality of the outcome when they are entered into willingly and with respect. To illustrate, we need merely to look at things like: birds eating insects of off larger mammals and reptiles, two plants sown close together that develop stronger root systems than one plant would alone, whales and their barnacles, the anemone and the clownfish, and the honeybee and the flower.

As discussed earlier, relationships can become a battleground if the masculine and feminine compete, rather than complete. It seems to me that in current society, the buried masculine that is struggling to recover its true power is not yet aware of its need for the divine feminine in tempering its power with grace and surrender. If the masculine (or male) does not realize this in a partnership, the tendency is to suppress the feminine power (or female) and compete against it (and her), instead of harmonizing and synergizing with it. The unaware male believes that to allow the feminine to emerge in its true power will envelope and erase him, rather than to enhance and compliment his own true power as a male. Here is where healing on the individual level and working with the divine masculine and feminine within oneself can bring the necessary awareness to a partnership and once again open the space for divine co-creation.

Healing on a Group Level (Healing in Families, Communities, and Businesses)

Healing on the partnership level as described above will provide the love, commitment, bonds, and structure necessary to radiate out to stronger relationships within the family unit, community groups, and businesses. Doing this work will undoubtedly have an effect on each member's sense of self-esteem and feelings of worthiness of their unique gifts. In addition, when healing work has been achieved by the majority of the group members, the ability to work in higher frequencies and greater resonance is achieved, and the quality of relationships, creations, and solutions to problems is exponentially increased. Family meetings will begin to look more like a Hawaiian Ho'oponopono session than the boring moments in time when one must simply endure a lecture from the mother or father as they scold or groan. Town hall meetings and community forums will have dramatically increased chances of successful outcomes that work for the good of all. Civic debates will become civic "dialogues" as all people will have a chance to be heard, and all ideas will be thrown in the pot for consideration. Community meetings will become "family meetings" where every member's well-being and quality of life is heard and considered. Government could once again become "for the people," as decisions are made in the highest frequency possible, in true cooperation with all of creation, bringing forth the highest good for all involved.

Families

In keeping with the theme of healing from the inside, out, our next logical step would be to examine the family unit. Let's begin by looking first at what a family is, and then at what its purpose is. If we look at it from the view of any other small group, be it in business, community groups, government, etc, it would seem that a "family" is a small group of people, with parents or caretakers of one kind or another at the helm. In these groups, everyone is expected to contribute in some way, and everyone benefits in some way. The "parents" (leaders, president, managers, governors, treasurers, org. team members, etc.), may provide a little extra energy in the form of: leadership, money, muscle power, wisdom, or energy—but all are part of a unit, and therefore a team. All members of the team contribute by doing such things as chores, paying membership fees, tasks either voluntary or assigned, etc. In this way, the common goal of a healthy family unit seems to be to incubate, develop, and nurture each person's dreams, projects, gifts, etc. so that all are supported towards giving their highest and shining their brightest in the world. As for what makes a family, it seems that anything goes. Today's families are put together in many different ways. They may consist of: two parent families, single parent families, step-parents, step-siblings, same-sex parents, grandparents rearing grandchildren, foster parents, adoptive parents, older siblings caring for the younger, and everything else you can imagine. As long as the members are healing, mentally and emotionally healthy, and supportive to each other, it is hard to argue that one type of family is really any better than another. Blood ties may create a family, but only intent, commitment, and communication can make a family, for family is based on connectedness and relatedness. To heal at the family and group level, it is imperative that we can begin to show up as our true selves, and that our deepest desires and soulful longings have a chance to be brought to the table and expressed. If most of the members within the family have done their individual and partnership level healing work, there is the potential for amazing cooperation within a family.

Each member of the family has their own unique gifts, traits, and talents. When the members are self-healed and whole enough to allow for these differences, and to listen to and respect all views, they will begin to see the rich treasures that are waiting to be revealed in these relationships. When men and women, individually as well as within their families, begin to find the courage to unearth the untruths created by society based on the illusion of separation and an imbalanced and worn out patriarchy, not only will they have to open up to healing themselves and finding new ways of being, but also to keeping their families in check when problems arise. If there is disharmony and discord, a healthy family will know to immediately bring the problem to the table and not to brush things under the rug, or if immediacy is not appropriate, to respect each other enough to find a more appropriate time and then to commit to showing up for each other.

I'd like to shed some light here on the ancient Hawaiian forgiveness and reconciliation practice of Ho'oponopono, as an example of the indigenous (feminine) wisdom that we are all one family, and when something is out of balance in one area, we are all affected. The Hawaiian word "pono" means "to make things right." When there is an imbalance in a Hawaiian family, a family elder or a community kahuna (priest) is called in to facilitate a healing and forgiveness session. The ancient Hawaiians, and those who continue this teaching, understood that it was unhealthy for individuals, families, and society to be out of balance or not "pono." They knew that what affected the individual affected the whole, and therefore always went straight to prayer, negotiation, truth telling, healing, and forgiveness for all parties affected. This feminine (nature and spiritually based) culture understood that to thrive in an earthly paradise we must live in balance with all things, and inner work and healing was the root of this balance.

The ancient indigenous culture in this example also understood that the children would immediately receive the effects of any unhealed energy between the family elders, parents, or older siblings. The lesson here is that there is much to be looked at in how our children are being raised. Are they being raised by conscious parents who have been able to do enough spiritual healing work on their own inner masculine and feminine, as well as their cultural imprints, to raise their children with more freedom than they had? Perhaps they are continuing what was passed on to them, without necessarily even realizing some of the repeating patterns or untruths that they are propagating? Only in healing the imbalance of the masculine and feminine within themselves at the individual level, and then the partnership level, can they begin to give their children a launching pad from a higher aspect than what they have been given.

Mothers and fathers who have not yet been able to uncover their true divine masculine and feminine or to fully integrate what they understand to be proper manifestations of a woman or man in their society will undoubtedly pass these things on to their children. Unconscious patterns, beliefs, and fears that have run rampant for many centuries will continue to be carried in the collective psyche until the timing is just right for a spiritual warrior with enough understanding of, or just lack of patience for what has not yet been brought to the surface, to go out looking for them and bring them home (within themselves and then to their families) for proper review. To be fair, most generations have made strides in some area or another to become healthier than the one before, although in some cases surely it has also been the opposite. Either way, so much of what is in our collective unconscious related to being male or female, our inner (or divine) masculine and feminine, and how we are to act within our culture if we are male or female—is solely a result of what those around us or our ancestors believed at the time. In order to induce change, anything that seems incongruent with a cooperative and authentic society must be properly looked at and either discarded, healed, or held onto as appropriate. We must be willing to look into where the incongruencies are within our families of origin, where our parents left us work to do, and get busy on our part.

Broken Families

When the unhealed aspects of the parents become larger than anyone can deal with, we may find the case of broken families. I believe that broken families may well be the biggest consequences of the traumas we've faced as a result of the extreme imbalance of the masculine and feminine. As an example, the absence of a healthy father figure, or even a father at all, has been a major barrier to healing and bringing the masculine and feminine to a center point. Families with unhealed mothers have been traumatized as well, but if we look at the larger picture, there appears to be a heavy absence of men from most broken families in the last century for sure.

This is huge. If the family incubator is not accurately supporting the proper development of a healthy masculine and feminine in its daughters and sons, it will leak over into a continuing imbalance for every future generation until it is looked at and healed. This will take courageous men and women who are willing to look into where their own divine masculine and feminine are imbalanced, where the untruths are in masculine and feminine ideals in society, and to teach their children a different way. Broken families where the masculine and feminine have been in competition have set the stage for a collective unwillingness to work together, co-create, and compromise. Where the partners have been unable to understand how to use the feminine to tap into the field of resonance (representative of the One-ness) to solve their issues, they have missed the support that exists to assist us in our crawl back from the fall into duality. When men or women are not willing to enter into self-inquiry through things like healing groups, counseling, or coaching because they have been taught that it must be "pretty bad" to have to do that or that "only crazy people go to counseling," they have missed an opportunity to learn from each other and continue to co-create beautiful things together.

Within that, however, there is also the issue of ineffective and even damaging coaching and counseling, which can further corrupt the willingness of many to delve again into that vulnerable arena without any reasonable guarantee of relief. As well, men in particular have been absent from the vast majority of self-help conferences and retreats, as they are still not generally supported by society overall in getting in touch with themselves or learning those things we don't learn in our masculine based school system—such as how to relate properly to one another. Another break occurs when only the women are willing to enter into counseling or the self-help arena, as they then tend to grow exponentially faster than the men. This many times leaves them unhappy with the quality of relationships that they are having with the men who are still unsupported and therefore hesitant to do the necessary work to learn the "feminine" world of relations and feelings. When they are unhappy with the quality of their relationships with their men due to their own rapid growth, this further inflames the men who are now feeling even more inferior to their women, and much more powerless. If society could just begin to support the men in making self-help "cool" and "manly," we may see a better outcome and much more satisfaction for both genders in their intimate relationships, families, and work lives. Think of it this way, women have discovered science and mathematics without any visible traumas; surely it's safe to start allowing the men to do the same in the realm of intuition and emotions.

If the above remedies are not catching on, and families remain broken, there is also the issue of how our society treats a couple when they do decide to part ways if they have indeed grown apart. When a relationship dissolves due to emerging differences in the desires, morals, vibrations, and visions of the partners, our society seeks to make someone "wrong" and therefore create a traumatic division between the two. This affects both the spiritual and emotional health of both partners, as well as any children involved, as they also begin to act this out with each other themselves. Again we see here how the out of balance patriarchy seeks to divide and compete rather than co-operate and complete. If we are able to apply more feminine principles of forgiveness, understanding, and reverence, we will see the gifts in these relationships and be able to foster hope and love in our children, rather than unforgiveness and vengeance. When we have achieved healthy families, we can then begin to examine how they support the community, the extended family, and the greater human family.

Communities

We all hunger for connection in our intimate relationships and families as well as our communities—the kind of connection where we can support and be supported, in all ways on all days. This is the beginning of democracy at its core—a world in which we support and are supported by all those around us, firmly rooted in connectedness and relatedness instead of separateness, elitism, or competition. In a real democracy, community groups exist to support the smaller family units. What would the world be like if one person from every family went back to ancient ways and began to serve again in their communities as representatives—those who report from their families to the larger whole what their needs are and how the larger community can best support them? We could go back to town hall meetings in the round, community dinners, festivals, and events that encourage relations between members of all of the different "families," rather than the isolation that sometimes occurs in the Western world when families traditionally keep to themselves or those they already know at these types of events. Community government could be re-structured to allow for a rotating panel of neighbors working on any given issue or project, or a plethora of other ideas. What it really comes down to, is that when we form any group, family, or community, and operate it from a baseline of intimacy, connection, teamwork and relatedness, supported first and foremost by a resonant field of acknowledged "oneness" within its members; we can begin to build sustainable family and community structures, and a world that works for all.

For example, what if, whenever there was an infraction outside of the family and in the greater community, we had a justice system that offered true healing, atonement, and reconciliation wherever possible for all parties involved? The #metoo, #timesup, #blacklivesmatter, etc. movements have brought to light the injustices to the keepers of the feminine energies that needed to be seen and acknowledged, but are missing the element of healing necessary to make a whole and workable system. In the majority of our current justice and social systems, wrongdoers (if they are prosecuted) are not only subject to punishment and reconciliation, but they may also face mass public shaming and the inability to ever again reclaim any semblance of a new life. Harmony is hard to restore under this system, as the wrongdoers will certainly fight with all that they have to be exempted from taking responsibility for their actions if there is no hope for transformation or forgiveness, and both victims and perpetrators have less opportunity to fully heal as the process never completes itself. The guilty party is punished (or not), but no atonement, reconciliation, or reflection is provided in most cases, and the victim has no sense of closure in most cases. If a guilty party knows that they will have to take responsibility for their actions, accept punishment, and atone, but that there is at least the possibility for healing on the other side of that road, perhaps hope can be restored on both sides.

Indigenous tribes that understood the value of harmony within the tribe knew that when a wrongful act was committed by one, that healing was needed on all ends of the spectrum. Again, the ancient Hawaiian ritual of Ho'oponopono is a good example of this. Justice in these groups was "restorative justice." The perpetrator was required to take responsibility for their actions and make amends, but both sides were also provided with true healing from other members of the tribe in order to bring back balance to the whole and "make things right" again. Restorative justice is to communities what Ho'oponopono is to families, in that it gives the offender and offended a chance to sit in moderation, atonement, reconciliation, and healing. Both parties must agree to the process, giving it an even greater chance of success.

In modern times, Ho'oponopono has been reduced to the mantra "I love you. I'm sorry. Please forgive me. Thank you," which is good in some applications. However, the ancient ritual is much more involved. A simple example lies in an act of wrongdoing within a family unit. When there was a wrong committed in a family, a mediator was brought in and no one was allowed to leave until healing and atonement had been achieved, and all members of the family accepted. In the process, the offended party was offered a chance to state the harm inflicted and what they desired in compensation, reconciliation, and amends. The offender then was afforded the chance to repair the harm by agreeing to amends, apologizing, and/or other transformational actions. Once reconciliation and a plan for atonement were achieved, both groups were required to break bread with one another and complete the cycle. The idea here is that everyone involved should be involved in the justice process, and that the justice process should lead to healing and repair of harm for ALL parties. It allows offenders to take responsibility for their actions, not just be sent through an isolating punishment system that often does little to address the reasons the person offended in the first place.

Restorative justice (which is said to have originated in indigenous Maori traditions- closely linked to indigenous Hawaiian traditions) is starting to be introduced into schools and justice systems, but we still have a long way to go to achieve true balance. The majority of our systems still do little to address the needs of the offended, in which case closure and the chance for true healing, forgiveness, and transformation for both parties is still unattended to. The point here is that continuing to point fingers or perpetuating perpetrator/victim consciousness will not bring peace, and this is not how we will heal as a society. Societal healing needs to include attention to all, and an understanding of why the pain is so strong. Hurt people, hurt people. Punishing the wrongdoers without investigating what caused their behavior, and locking them up or ostracizing them from society via public shaming of any type does not solve the problem. In order to break the cycle, truths and wrongs need to be brought into the light, but the wrong-doers also need to be allowed to take responsibility for their actions, atone, and be healed, rather than solely being shunned, shamed, or cut off from their fellow humans forever. In the greater picture, this only perpetuates the wheel of anger, shame, fear, and more wrong-doing within society. When we can allow some of the indigenous cultures' ideals to cooperate with our Western ideals, we will once again understand that we are all connected, and will develop more and more programs, habits, rituals and rites that support that connection.

Restorative justice and the healing of the masculine and feminine on all levels is where societal healing begins. The shadows have risen massively to the surface at this time to be brought into the light. Will we heal them on a global scale, or point fingers and cast these atrocities back into the shadows? Dismantling the oppressive out of balance patriarchy will take more than just ruining the careers and reputations of a few high profile perpetrators. We must go deeper, and make it o.k. for men and boys to feel and to heal, while we allow for women to stand in their rightful power.

Part Four

Beginning to Heal

"The Microcosm Flows to the Macrocosm"

Healing ourselves, our partnerships, families, groups, and communities will organically affect the resonant field and collective consciousness, thereby changing our memes (ideas, behaviors, styles, or usage that spreads from person to person within a culture). As we heal from the inside, out beginning with ourselves, our partnerships, our families, and our communities, anything that happens on the greater stage (the macrocosm) will be a direct reflection our inner states (the microcosm). In the past, individuals as well as society have desperately attempted to make the outside reflect the inside, by quickly applying solutions and more control to the imbalances. As we've now seen, the path to real and sustainable peace is just the opposite, and occurs from the inside out.

Therefore, one person can make a difference, provided we all learn to see ourselves as important pieces of the whole, who, when joined together in perfect harmony and collective resonance, can affect the macrocosm in dynamic ways. In healing the masculine and feminine, it is ALL about relationships. Working on our relationships with ourselves, our partners, our families, and our communities will allow us to create sacred containers strong enough to hold what wants to emerge from the depths of our souls and the grace of God/that which is greater than us. I strongly believe it is best to focus on connections to our higher power, ourselves, and each other from our hearts. For in our vulnerability and authenticity, we are able to deal with each other, our problems, etc. at a real level, with no masks, and without fear, and THERE will we find our true power—stripped down to the core, and starting from there. Not everyone will agree with this, and not everyone will like who they become when they do discover their true self, but relating to each other on that level is a necessary step in order for any real healing to be possible.

If we are choosing a world that works for everyone, where everyone is honored and supported for their unique gifts and talents, looking into our wounds and walking into our shadows is a necessary step. Through individual healing, partnership healing, family healing, and group healing, we become less aware of our separateness, and more aware of the unique features each of us have brought to the table. It is then that we will truly create magnificent relationships, as well as all of the outer manifestations of our talents that make our world both easier to navigate, as well as infinitely more beautiful. When we are able to walk into the shadows, face our demons, and eradicate them one by one, healing our individual and collective traumas and shadows can open a space for interdependence, a larger collective field of abundance and creativity, and equal sharing and caring caused by a newly built foundation of reverence for all life.

Patriarchal society has done a blessed job in finding solutions to our everyday "problems." Through masculine energy, we have done a great job of figuring out how to "survive." Thriving, however, is the next logical step in our journey on earth. It involves a spiritual component, which, though acknowledged in the past, has been steered into patriarchal based religions, which have also become out of balance, and in some instances completely out of touch with genuine spirituality. Thriving, which involves a holistic approach of meaningful work, play, and relationships, is something that cannot be "worked on" or "fixed" with a solution rooted in divine masculine energy, and is therefore not solvable in our current state of being in Western culture.

Feminine principals of relating, sharing, and witnessing each other are as equally important to a "survive and thrive" mentality as masculine principles of solutions and fact finding. In fact, if there is no thriving, there also may be no surviving. Consider the many studies of what happened to babies that weren't touched, and animals and humans that have died of grief. To live and not thrive is to die a slow death of the soul, which may become more frightening than physical death. To acknowledge and therefore release the fear of physical death is to open up to the bounty of living fearlessly—and is found within thriving human relationships with the self and others.

It stands to be seen that all human commerce requires relationships anyway—therefore proving the impossible inseparability of masculine and feminine principals of solutions and relations in the worlds of business, logic, and industry. We in Western society have over-honed our skills of science, industry, logic, and left-brain thinking. To move forward, the keepers of the masculine must step back and be willing to listen, and the keepers of the feminine must step forward and teach what they have to give. Men may not be given permission by other men and a patriarchal society to listen, learn, and integrate feminine principals of relating. Therefore, courageous men (and women) must step forward fully into themselves and their humbleness and feebleness, as well as their wholeness and perfections, and be willing to encourage and inspire each other. The change starts from within. For each person willing to risk becoming humble and learning a new way—a thousand more will be inspired. Society will begin to change from the inside, out (feminine) rather than from the outside, in (masculine) while still retaining all of the form, function, and benefit of masculine principles of life and society.

There is a reason why we cannot go entirely back to the old ways of strictly matriarchal societies. We have tasted the benefits of masculine machines, inventions, and beauty. We will only be satisfied and set free when we bring the matriarchal values that we lost up to the speed of our current century and lifestyle. It is then that we will truly thrive.

Resources for Beginning to Heal

In addition to offering an examination on how the masculine and feminine have gotten out of balance and how they can begin to heal, I wanted to also offer some practical tools. In this section I would like to offer my suggestions for resources to those who would like to undertake the journey of individual, partnership, group, and collective healing—to provide all who have read this book with enthusiasm and inspiration next steps in how to become catalysts in this massive change in consciousness.

Section One

General- For the First Three Levels of Healing

At the Individual Level

Before embarking on healing on the individual level, we should first stop to recognize and acknowledge our true courage as a spiritual warrior! Getting to know ourselves and eradicating the mind and soul of the many untruths we have absorbed is great work. As so many of these untruths based in the original fall into duality and consequent illusion of separation are deeply rooted in our psyches, they will take persistence and perseverance to uncover and transform. Beginning to work with a gifted counselor, psychotherapist, life coach, or holistic healer can help greatly as one goes through this process. This would also be an appropriate time to turn to: books, spiritual groups, meditation or an inner stillness practice, as well as a variety of other self-help or spiritual journeying tools. Turning to a higher power first, and then following the guidance given (ensuring the guidance is benevolent and not ego-based) toward the things that are uniquely best for us is of course, even better. All that is needed is to simply listen to our inner voice, and then follow what feels right. All else will begin to unfold from there. As each spiritual warrior has the courage and support to hit the bumps, potential backlash from others, and repeating patterns head on, these courageous souls will begin to transform their relationships with others and the world itself as deeper and more authentic relationships with others slowly become the new norm. If you are one of them—how brave you are!

Exercises for Knowing Yourself

Meditation

If you already know how to meditate, great! Get to it—you know how much it helps your overall balance, groundedness, and relationship with yourself and others. If you have never meditated before, however, let me offer some guidance. Now here's the deal—I am not going to say what everyone else says about how to do it "properly." You do not have to sit in a pretzel pose, spend a certain amount of time doing it, or do it in a certain way. And if your mind won't shut off so you can be in a mindless state, don't worry! I usually suggest guided meditations to beginners. It gives your mind something to do, and it is a great way to learn to meditate. You will not be checking the clock, trying to rid your head of pesky thoughts, or otherwise judging yourself for not doing it "right." You can grab many guided meditations on cd, digitally, or even record your own. Allow a soothing voice to talk you through some lovely imagery, and don't worry if you're not imaging it correctly. Every person will have their own experience; the speaker's offerings are a merely a guide to get you started. When you have used the guided meditations long enough, you may be ready to try meditating on your own. My advice? Don't time yourself or force yourself. Just sit, close your eyes, and be still. You don't even need to focus on your breath if that throws you off. Remember also that there are many ways to meditate, including moving meditations or zoning out while listening to music on headphones. Just do what works for you, because that's what helps.

Journaling

There are many ways to go about this as well. Some prefer to do it "diary style" and recap their day or just write out their feelings. You can also try it "automatic writing style" which would involve asking yourself questions on paper and allowing your pen or fingers on the keyboard to give you the answers via your higher self/intuition/higher power. In this case, you just relax, get your mind out of the way, and open up to whatever wants to be typed or written. You can go underneath each layer of your question to get to the core of the issue by asking, "And why do I feel that way?" after each answer until you find a root cause.

Working With a Life Coach or Therapist

Before I start this section, I have an important recommendation for you. When searching for a life coach or therapist to work with, please check out the provider's website, chat with them for a little bit if you are able, and then use your intuition. A life coach or therapist should make you feel empowered, not awful. My other suggestion is that they should be working to be un-employed by you—that is to say they should help you find your own answers, work with you until you have more clarity, and then let you go unless you need check-ins here and there. They should not make you feel bad about yourself or like you'll need them forever. You are looking to level up your life, clear out any blocks, and create healing so you can understand yourself better and show up for life as more of who you truly are in order to give your gifts to the world. The point of working with one of these professionals is not to dig up your story just to keep throwing it around—but to use it for information, healing, and insight, and then to release what no longer serves you. Be sure to do your homework and go with a coach or counselor who makes you feel inspired and empowered. There are far too many counselors still practicing in our Western system who do much more harm than good.

Books/Retreats/Classes/Etc.

Either in-person or online, a retreat, class, book, or gathering that is focused on finding and developing your inner self is a great tool for self-understanding and self-healing.

Bodywork/Hypnosis/Energy Healing/Etc.

Massage, yoga therapy, hypnosis, energy healing, etc. are all very powerful in pulling up old hurts and wounds, releasing them, and transforming yourself and your life.

Note The examples listed above are for maintenance.

If you have been triggered and there is something that needs to be looked at in order for you to grow or learn something, you will have to ramp up these techniques in order to find what you need. Practicing what one of my clients dubbed "fear sitting" is a great option here. You simply sit in a chair and allow the undesirable feeling to wash over you for two minutes. It may feel like two hours, but after about thirty seconds, the feeling will start to release its hold on you because you are giving it your attention. If you are in the middle of being triggered and can't get yourself to a safe and quiet space in order to journal, meditate, or fear sit, breathe through it the best that you can and promise yourself that you will come back to work with it at a later time, and then do so.

In general you must learn to be comfortable with being uncomfortable for a little while in order to pull up old untruths and find out who you really are. This takes away most of the resistance, and makes the process that much easier. Western society has a real aversion to being uncomfortable, and we pride ourselves on trying to make the sensation go away by any means possible. In order to truly heal ourselves, our world, and the masculine and feminine in all that is, we must change this perception and embrace the gifts to be found in being uncomfortable.

In the midst of getting to know yourself, you must also learn to love yourself. Truly loving yourself gives you the best possible advantage to loving and supporting other people, your community, and the planet. Healthy, happy people who love themselves are magnets for others who are doing the same. The more whole people there are, the better we all are.

Exercises for Loving Yourself

Feed Your Mind, Body, and Soul with Healthy Things

Eating healthy foods, exercising, keeping yourself balanced, making decisions that are healthiest for your mind, body, and spirit, and doing things that feed your soul are so important. These are the keys to balancing your physical life with your spiritual life. Be sure that you have some sort of practice to engage with whatever you know is bigger than you, whatever that looks like to you. If you love art, make art. If you love to dance or sing, do that, just for the fun of it. Play, laugh, have fun. Another way Western society has gotten sorely out of balance is with the idea that to "do" is more important than to "be." It most certainly is not, and when we entertain the masculine energy of "doing" without the proper balance of "being," everything about our lives becomes off balance and un-sustainable. So don't worry about doing more necessarily (unless that is something you need to do to love yourself). As you find ways to love yourself and become more open, playful, and flowing, you will find yourself a lot more willing to "do" the things you need and want to do anyway.

Give Yourself Grace

Give yourself grace when you think you've made a mistake. When the critical voices go off in your head, treat yourself as you would treat a friend who was saying those things out loud about themselves. You wouldn't let your friend say a bunch of negative things about themselves, so love yourself as much as you would your friend. A quick tip—if a negative thought enters your head, find something to be grateful for. This will immediately shift the negative thought into something much more nurturing of your being.

Be Kind to Yourself

Remind yourself of all the things you've done right! Grab a piece of paper and keep it in your purse, wallet, or somewhere where you'll see it every day. Write the sentence: "I am proud of myself for: ________" and then fill in the blank. Do this for 21 days (the amount of time it takes to create a new habit) and see how the chatter in your head changes. Throughout your day, every time you see it, fill in the blank for yourself. Spend more time reminding yourself of everything you've done right, rather than beating yourself up for everything you think you've done wrong. We are our own biggest critics, and being mean and judgmental to ourselves makes it far too easy to do the same to others. A bad attitude towards ourselves can accidentally leak out to those around us.

Forgive Yourself

It is far too easy to find yourself ruminating over things in your head that you think you should have done differently or better and you're having a hard time letting go of. Instead of keeping yourself locked in a cage that you refuse to allow yourself to escape from as punishment for your "bad deeds," try instead asking yourself a simple question. "If someone else did this exact same thing in this exact same situation, would I forgive them?" If your answer is immediately "yes," then you know what you need to do.

Why is it so hard to forgive ourselves, when we would forgive others much more easily? I'm not sure, perhaps it has to do with so many years of messages from authority figures saying how "bad" we are. Either way, in order for us to heal as a species and as a planet, we're going to have to find a way to turn that around. So many of the infractions we feel we cannot let ourselves off the hook from are minor, and would be forgiven and forgotten so easily if they were coming from someone outside of ourselves. Again, since what we do to ourselves can leak out into the way we treat others (even unconsciously) we need to address this infraction we are inflicting upon ourselves. Unforgiveness of ourselves and others can lead to a life lived in a less than vibrant state, due to pain, dis-ease, unhealthy relationships and choices, or any other manifestation that occurs. If you find yourself stuck in a pattern of doing this in your head or otherwise, again, you can pattern-interrupt those thoughts. Stop when you notice it and ask yourself, "What have I done that's really awesome?" "What am I really proud of myself for?" Again, this will immediately change the energy of the block you are creating in your head or otherwise. In order to create any change or healing for yourself or anyone around you, as well as for the world at large, you must learn to forgive yourself in order to allow this healing to take place. If you don't, you are essentially saying "I'm not worthy of moving forward," and in that case, no amount of wishing or trying to go forward is going to actually work. There's a better way, and you can't move forward in creating anything new and more beautiful without it.

Re-framing "Failures"

When you try to do something and don't succeed, instead of beating up on yourself, try re-framing things. Failures are really just opportunities for the right things to work out later. If you keep trying to manifest something or plan something and the door keeps getting shut in your face, you have not failed. You tried something, you took steps towards it and you thought it was going to work. If it didn't, it just means that you don't have it quite right yet. It's not your fault. We aren't supposed to know everything.

If you are having a hard time with this, try thinking of the metaphor of the inventor. An inventor by nature has to fail repeatedly before they come upon the one amazing invention that changes the world. That's how they refine what they are inventing so that it works in the best way possible. So if whatever steps you have taken: spiritual, emotional, physical, etc. toward what you are trying to manifest haven't worked, you haven't failed. You've just come one step closer to the exact formula or the exact mix of things that will work. Try seeing a failure as an opportunity to try different, try harder, etc. If you beat up on yourself, you just put yourself back in that cage and told yourself you aren't worthy. If you deem yourself unworthy, you hold yourself back from the world, and we need you to be your full self in order to heal the collective. Your relationships and the world need you to be your whole self. Holding yourself back only starves yourself, the people around you, as well as the world of your gifts. Reframing your failures should help you to understand that the more you get up and keep trying, the more courageous you are. If you keep getting up every time the door gets slammed in your face or everything falls apart, you have all the reason in the world to celebrate yourself for this fact.

At the Partnership Level

Again, working with a gifted marriage and family therapist, life coach, or spiritual counselor can be of great help at this level. There are also many books, courses, support groups, and workshops available to those who have done their work individually and now wish to expand their healing to their intimate partnerships. The healing circles and leaderless church discussed later are also great ways to deepen this healing. For now, here are some tried and true tips I've used with couples that most people have never been taught, but work like a charm when fully embraced.

Don't Make Promises You Can't Keep, Make Promises You Find Achievable

When your partner asks something of you, don't say yes to something you will later feel resentful for. This is especially important when you are tempted to do something solely to make your partner happy. As discussed earlier, even though it is counter-intuitive to our culture that teaches us to make everybody else happy before we make ourselves happy, we actually need to make ourselves happy first. The other person is not responsible for your inner happiness. If you do things you know you don't want to you are bound to create resentment, and anything that creates resentment is equal to poison in a relationship. If you've already had times that you felt resentful or realized that you were doing things that you probably shouldn't have said yes to, or if you've tried to manipulate your partner into feeling like they "made you" do something—understand that our partners don't make us do anything. Hopefully we are in the relationship of our own free will and in that, we are agreeing or not agreeing to things in every moment. In a healthy partnership you talk those things out. That's why it's so important to learn to know and love yourself first—so that you are brave enough to come to the table and kindly and lovingly say these things to your partner, as well as to trust in the other person that they can handle it.

There is a caveat to all of this, however, and that is to not promise the person nothing either. So again, don't make promises you can't keep, but be able to understand yourself well enough to know what promises you can make, and then hold yourself accountable for those. Your partner has to know that they can count on you for some things, so choose things you know you are o.k. with. There need to be some things that are reasonable enough for your partner to trust that they can count on you for.

To further illustrate this concept, let's look at a quick and easy example. Say your partner asks you to go to a violent or action packed movie. Now, knowing yourself well, you know that this type of movie will make you feel drained and heavy, and that it will not be a fun experience. If your partner really wants to see the movie and you say "yes," they will most likely feel you recoiling at the experience, and then they aren't going to have any fun anyway. They would probably have had more fun if they went on their own, or with another friend that likes those types of movies. It's even possible you could have a conflict as your partner will be feeling let down, and you will be feeling drained, heavy, and out of sorts. The other thing to notice here is that a movie is entertainment. You would be choosing this for fun, not because it's something that has to be done or seems like it has to be done. In this example, and in a partnership where both partners are conscious, it is going to be far better if you trust your partner to be able to handle your truth. And feel free to give the whole truth. Try something like "I really want to go with you, but I'm afraid I won't feel well watching that type of movie, and I don't want you to have a bad time. Why don't you go with your friend? I would love to do something else with you." You can see how this is a much more loving answer, and will most likely have a better outcome than if you said yes, and then maybe tried to blame your partner later when you aren't feeling good. Your partner can only take you at your word. If you say you are o.k. with something, it is reasonable for them to accept your truth. If that is not your truth, it is up to you to tell it and not to assume your partner should know or can guess.

When we show up in our full truth and trust our partners with it, relationships become much more intimate as the trust grows, and both parties know exactly what is on the table. This is the way to a healthy partnership. The more you trust them with your truth, the closer together you feel—even though again, society has had us thinking the opposite for many years.

If Promises are Broken

In the event that you promise your partner something that you thought you could reasonably do and for whatever reason you aren't able to fulfill, you will need to address that immediately. In other words "if the game changes, change the game plan." Perhaps your schedule changed and you can no longer fulfill your obligation. Whatever it is, if something changes, be respectful enough to come to the table and talk to your partner to renegotiate and see where they are at with the issue. Perhaps there is an easy solution. Though you don't want to say yes to things you can't deliver, or may no longer be able to give something you previously promised, your partner should be able to count on you for some things—so be willing to renegotiate, and give where you can.

Not Leaving the Table Until Everyone Is Happy

Whenever you and your partner have differing ideas about something that needs to be decided, do yourselves the favor of coming up with a plan that feels good for everyone. If that takes a bit, so be it. As you can see from the previous examples, you never want to do something for someone else that you don't really want to, as it will breed resentment and have a negative effect on the relationship. "Giving in" is not a good negotiation tactic, unless you can truly wrap your head around being o.k. with it. If not, keep searching for a more favorable solution, so everyone feels honored and like they got a fair shake.

In an out of balance patriarchy heavily rooted in competition rather than cooperation, there has been a feeling of "if you win, I lose," or vice versa, rather than "everyone wins." It doesn't need to be that way, and we can work towards changing it. An easy example to consider is being on vacation and bartering with a craftsman from that town that is selling souvenirs. Let's say they don't have a specific price, and you have to negotiate. What feels good in a barter situation? When both people walk away feeling like they got a great deal! If you were to buy something from that person when you know that you worked them over really hard and they didn't want to say yes, (maybe they just did it to get rid of you or something), I can't imagine it would feel really good to have that handmade item. What feels really good is when we both honor ourselves and the other person. Though this is a casual example, you can see that if this is the best cause of action with people we only interact with once, then of course we will want to do the same with those closest to us! Though this is an easy example, know that when the stakes are higher (say your partner is considering a job offer in another state), there are going to be a lot of feelings to consider and a lot to discuss. Both parties may need to do their own inner work to search their heart and find their real feelings about the issue. You may need to go back to the individual exercises and ask yourself questions and get underneath your true feelings. When each of you does your own work, you can come back to the conversation in a loving, honoring manner and treat your partner's feelings, dreams, and ideas as kindly as you hopefully do your own.

Do yourself, your partner, and your relationship a favor and hold the space for that conversation for as long as is needed until everyone feels honored and respected and can agree on something. Again, don't leave the table until everyone is happy, even if it takes a little longer. Make sure to keep the conversation open and try putting it on the "side burner" in your mind for awhile. This way it's not right in front of your face all of the time, but you haven't forgotten about it either. Sometimes the time in-between a larger decision gives people even more time to sit on things and come up with new ideas or search their feelings a little deeper. When you've put it on the side burner and it's in your awareness but you are going about your everyday things, in many cases, that "a ha" moment can happen when you're doing something mundane and not thinking about it at all, such as taking a shower or doing the dishes.

Trust

Trust is one of the most important things in a healthy partnership. When you feel safe with someone, your opportunity to create and explore your world both inside and out is given a safe container in which to roam. You will feel peaceful in your relationship, and your overall life anxiety will be greatly reduced. One of the top ways to develop trust in a relationship is to develop healthy boundaries. You want to make sure that you are outlining those healthy boundaries for yourself, but also need to make sure your partner understands what they are. In the best case scenario, you want to be sure that everyone understands each other's boundaries before they get crossed.

If there are some things that you understand to be your "no's" from getting to know yourself, you should share them with your partner at some point. If one of your "no's" gets crossed, make sure that you are firm, but also loving and kind as you tell your partner that that is one of your "no's" and it's not o.k. for them to cross that line. Make sure that you do this early on so that your partner understands that this is a serious boundary of yours, that you aren't going to be wishy-washy about it, and that it's not o.k. to cross it. This type of behavior is actually respectful on both ends as your partner doesn't have to guess what your boundaries are, and you are confident in what is non-negotiable behavior for people to display towards you. This is not to be used so much for easy things, but for your strong no's—things that are absolutely non-negotiable for you. It's always best to have everyone on the same page as early on as possible to avoid messy entanglements when people are unaware of other's needs and boundaries.

The Fun Stuff!

Plan together, dream together, and play together. These things are essential to a healthy partnership. When the more challenging things come along, it's best to have a solid foundation of love, fun, and connection that is constantly being created alongside the rest of life that is happening. So cultivate this often, both in advance of any potential changes as well as during any changes.

To dream together—find out what's important to both of you and get on the same page. To play together—go on dates, dance in the kitchen, go to the park, talk, and enjoy life in whatever way feels good in every moment.

Balance and Maintenance

Just like a garden, a relationship needs regular watering, weeding, attention, and love. Balance the talks, negotiations, and inner-work with play, and pay attention to all of it regularly. Remember as well the priority this relationship takes in your life. You can't just work all of the time or worry all of the time and expect your relationship to be o.k. You must remember your priorities and why you got together with this person in the first place. Most people will count their relationships as their highest priorities in life, so be sure that you are working to live and not living to work, and that you are giving your important relationship the attention it deserves as a top priority in your life.

A good example to help you look at priorities is a hierarchy: at the top is your relationship with whatever you understand to be bigger than you, under that is your relationship with yourself, next is a relationship with a partner (intimate relationship), after that is your relationship with your kids if you have them, and after that is work. If you reverse these, you will put all of your energy into making work or something else the most important, and your foundational pieces are going to suffer. The foundational pieces have to be the strong bricks in place to support the rest of it. Jobs can come and go, different worries or stresses you have are going to come and go. If you are trying to create a healthy partnership, you have to maintain that and make it a high priority right after what's bigger than you and yourself. If you expect it to be there and sustain itself, it won't survive, because it needs to be fed.

If you are being pressured to give more energy to your job, etc. but you know that you're out of balance and are ignoring yourself, your higher power, or your partner, you won't be able to sustain that for very long. If there's something that is a true emergency that you need to give a little extra energy for a little while and everyone around you knows that you will be back right after you give the other thing your full attention that is different. Just be sure you remain diligent during this time. If you slowly begin to shift your priorities and attention to constantly attending to work, money, etc. in the wrong priority order, it will take its toll. Just as your job won't be there if you don't go to it, your relationship won't be there if you ignore it for a long time.

Another thing important for balance is to look to see if you have any unnecessary "time gobblers." These would be things that are taking up your time that you don't necessarily have to be doing, and aren't contributing to the health of your mind, body, and spirit. See if there are places where you can shave some of those off, and then do so. Remember also that a relationship is a feminine energy and therefore more abstract, and work is a masculine energy and is tangible. So a relationship may look different as it's hard to see any specific things you need to do to maintain it, whereas your job may spell out exactly what you need to do. A relationship has to be honored, maintained, and given to in a feminine energy. This includes things like support, caring, love, holding space, and the feelings that you are getting across.

When Challenges Arise

If (and when) challenges arise (as they will because anything worth doing will have its challenges), there are some things you will need to remember. The first thing you will want to do is stop and ask yourself some questions. If something goes wrong in your partnership and you aren't getting what you need, ask yourself what it is that you actually want. Perhaps your partner can't give it to you because you're not even sure what it is. Maybe you have an old wound that's being triggered.

Next, ask yourself if you have any blocks to receiving what it is that you want. Again, if an old wound is being triggered, you may need to look at what belief you may have taken on when the original event occurred. Perhaps there was a time in your life that you told yourself, "Well, I'm never going to get that anyway, so I'm just not going to want it," or "I'm going to compensate for the fact that I'm not going to get that and it hurts by being perfect, being mean, and making everything a joke," or any other coping mechanism you may have been using. Going back and digging up the original wound will help you understand how you are feeling about the present situation.

Next, you want to ask yourself if what you want is reasonable given the situation, your partner, yourself, and all of the other current details. The following question would be, "Is there anything I can do to help with this situation and get myself closer to the relationship that I want?" This is a good time to go to your higher power, journal, or meditate to find out your true feelings. Another good question to ask yourself is "Why do I want this?" Do you want it because it's something that you want to create, you're passionate about it, and it's important to you, or is it possible that underneath your desire is a fear you are trying to compensate for? An example would be if you have a fear of not having enough money. Perhaps you insist on doing certain things to make money or to be sure there is a good flow of money. In this example, you would want to stop and ask yourself why you want more money. Do you just want to create more money and you don't really have any pangs around it—or are you really afraid of not having enough money and the issue is important to you because you are trying to compensate for a fear? These are just examples, as there could be issues with fear of abandonment or anything else that may have shown up earlier in your life that you may be trying to compensate for.

Then you can test yourself. Ask yourself, "Will my life be better, will I be healthier, and will my relationship be healthier if I have it?" If so, why, and will everything still be o.k. without it?

After you've sat with these questions for awhile, you can then approach your partner to have a very clear conversation about what you're feeling and where your heart is. In that way, you can work out a better negotiation on whether it's best to solve your problem immediately or not. Sometimes it's not best to solve your problem immediately as there may be a reason this block is in your way. If your partner comes in to save you, you may actually be missing a lesson that is important to your growth or the health of the relationship that you would miss if it was immediately solved. In these cases, it's best to hold space for your partner and yourself in order to have the opportunity to grow stronger and learn a lesson that may just come up again if it isn't looked at and understood. It may be best to hold some space for awhile until the lesson can be gained, even if it's uncomfortable. Again, this may seem counter-intuitive to what we were taught, but it is very worth looking at in a different way.

Venting- "Passing the Poison"

I do not believe in venting. I believe venting is a by-product of a victim and blame culture where taking responsibility for changing our own behavior, the things around us, or stepping into our challenges is not encouraged. True venting is just passing the poison. If you come directly from a highly charged situation where either you have been triggered, or someone else got triggered and dumped it on you, you have not yet had the time to work with it internally and bring that energy down. In this situation, all that venting would accomplish is to take all of the intense and negative energy you just absorbed and immediately pass it on to your unsuspecting partner.

Many people think it makes them feel better to vent, but it really doesn't. If you vent, you haven't dealt with an opportunity you had learn and grow. Instead, because you were uncomfortable, you tried to get it off of you as quickly as possible and dumped it on someone else. Even if someone else dumped the negativity on you, you don't want to pass the poison to your partner. Your partner is the person that's always there for you, that you love, cherish, and respect. It's not good to vent to them when you're feeling highly charged, as it doesn't help the situation anyway.

Unless it's an emergency, sit with yourself first and bring down that energy. Journal, talk to your higher power, ask yourself some questions to figure out what happened, or just be still for awhile. After you have brought down the energy, if you are still missing some pieces or want to bounce it off of someone, approach your partner at another time as your best friend, and ask them if they are willing to work on it with you so you can further understand what happened. In that way, the energy is brought way down, and things can actually be figured out—as healthy communication is not possible in a high energy state anyway. When you can bring your energy down, you can be clear about what may actually need to be responded to.

Resentment

There is no place for resentment in a healthy relationship. It is poison and will only counteract anything you're doing to create a healthy relationship. Imbuing a relationship with resentment would be like trying to grow a beautiful garden while throwing bombs in it every day. You wouldn't expect the soil or harvest to be healthy if you were poisoning it every day. Be sure to do what you can to get to the bottom of any resentful feelings you have. Most likely they are coming from old programs in your head, a way that you are out of alignment with yourself, or some way that you tried to fix or save your partner instead of allowing them to do their own inner work. If you are trying to people-please, have the courage to say what you need to say or do what you need to do in a loving manner.

Projecting

If you are feeling angry at your partner, check with yourself first to see if somehow you may have unconsciously set your partner up to look like they did something wrong when the issue is really within you. In reality, because you may have always thought your life would look a certain way, you may have acted unconsciously in a way that brought you a repeating pattern you expected, but then blamed your partner for it instead.

Look Deeper

Hopefully you have some type of ongoing relationship with something that is bigger than you. When you are struggling, always look deeper than what is on the surface. This is a good time to go to this higher power to ask some questions to find out where you are missing things. It's almost impossible to do this all completely on your own, especially when challenges arise, so remember to go to your support systems, physical and non-physical for support.

See the Good

In order to build anything healthy and good, you need to first see it that way. Do everything you can to remind yourself that what you are creating or have created is healthy and good. Focus on what is working, rather than what isn't. When you have challenges and also when you don't, focus your energy on what is working. We tend to focus on the negative in our own heads or things we hear from others rather than all of the good that exists. Our brains believe the negative more easily, so we actually have to work to keep the positivity going—but it's so worth it when it helps us to see our creations through all of their seasons.

What are all of the awesome things you have brought to your relationship? What have you done really well on your end? What has your partner contributed and done really well? What's positive about your relationship? What does it bring to everyone around you, and what ripple effects does it create? Remember to focus just as much (if not more) energy on what is going well, than on the challenges you are facing.

Exercise

My partner is awesome at: ______________________ Or: My future partner is awesome at:____________________, and fill in the blank. In doing this simple exercise, your focus will begin to lean towards all of the awesome things that your partner does and is and it will fill your life with more of the same.

Repeating Issues

What happens when you have worked with yourself and your partner, perhaps about a boundary, and things haven't changed? How does one change? Normally, you have a discussion about something, someone apologizes and then says "I will work on that." This often manifests in a few days or maybe a week of trying to be kinder, nicer, or consider the issue. Most likely, after a short amount of time goes by, you or they will slip because it's a habit. When you say "I will work on it," what you should really mean is that you will work towards adopting a new habit. It takes at least twenty-one days for a new habit to form when your default behavior has been something else. It takes this long to adopt new neural pathways in your brain so that when the same situation presents itself, you will respond from a new habit rather than what has been ingrained in you for a long time. Instead of saying "I will work on that" and imagining that you will just consider the issue often in your mind, plan to take concrete steps toward building the new habit that you would like to adopt. This not only gives you a greater chance for success in changing the habit, but allows your partner to truly see that you are "working on it" in a tangible manner.

Exercises

Write it Down

Email or text your partner a certain sentiment every day to keep yourself in the mindset of the new habit you want to create, write yourself notes to remind yourself, read a book every day on the subject, or do any other tangible thing you can think of that will help you create a new habit. Develop at least one ritual per day that puts yourself in the vibration of the thing you wish to create. The act of writing it down also allows you to think in positive terms about what you DO want rather than what you don't wish to do anymore, so you can be sure you are spending your energy towards that which you do wish to create.

Gratitude Practice

Another way you can keep your relationship healthy and in a high vibration is to cultivate a gratitude practice. It's not difficult, and the awesome thing is that once you've focused on it during the time you've set aside for it, you will find that you end up with more reverence for life at all times of the day. This is a wonderful thing. When you go about your day, you will begin to find gratitude and awe in things you encounter that you may previously have taken for granted. You will begin to hear the birds, smell the grass, and taste your food with a higher sensitivity for how amazing everything is.

There are a few different ways to cultivate a gratitude practice. If you like to see things on paper, you can keep a gratitude journal. My favorite way is to do my "five things" before bed. Before I go to sleep at night, I stop and think about at least five things that I am grateful for from that day. Most days it's more than five, but trust me, you can always find at least five. If you're breathing, that's one. If you've had a meal, you've already got two, no matter what kind of challenging day you've had. When you put yourself in the vibration of gratitude, your relationship will be in that vibration and it will be much easier to attract the things that you desire, and everything will work a little bit better. If you tend to be a pessimist or complain, it will be hard to attract what it is you desire because you've told the universe that you don't believe it's possible. When you and your partner do this together at night, it creates even more harmony and possibilities for creation in your relationship.

Above all, remember why you want your relationship, why you got into it, and how important it is to you. This will help you be willing to do the things it takes to maintain it, just like changing the oil in your car. You want your car to run and take you where you need to go, and you appreciate having it to make life nicer and more fulfilling. To change your car's oil is to give it regular maintenance. Since great relationships are one life's greatest treasures, it should be easy to recognize the importance of the daily love, care, and maintenance they require.

At the Family Level

A family that recognizes and honors its member's needs, desires, and personalities while remembering to honor each person's role will find great harmony. The respect, honor, and kindness that are cultivated on the individual and partnership level will surely extend to family interactions as well—so paying attention to these levels first will pay great dividends when cultivating good family relations.

The healthiest families, in my opinion, are the ones where the parents or caregivers understand that their role is to do their own inner work in cooperation with their higher power and other appropriate adults, professionals, or groups, while serving as guides for their children. The family container is healthiest when the caregivers continually work to balance and heal their own inner masculine and feminine, allowing them to provide strong energetic containers for their children's emotional growth. This attention to inner work by the parents enables the children to explore their own relationships to themselves and the world around them in a nurturing environment, lessens the amount of healing required on their parts as adults, and allows them the best chance of creating a more balanced future for generations to come.

Family healing techniques that may be helpful include things like the aforementioned practice of Ho'oponopono, Non-Violent Communication practices, family therapy, parent groups, counseling, workshops, community groups for families, and many more. One need merely look into a community directory for descriptions and listings of resources that most resonate. If nothing you find sounds good to you, feel free to create your own! With the ease of the internet in creating groups and meet-ups, the sky is the limit!

As the details of family life can be quite complex, and the focus of the majority of my work as an author, speaker, holistic life coach, healer, and wedding officiant is to discuss the healing of the masculine and feminine—I am choosing to leave this section open-ended. My point is simply that to heal on the outside, we must begin the healing on the inside, and radiate out from there. I wish you well in delving into the family healing tools that work best for you and your family—and all of the different situations and personalities therein.

Section Two

Bringing it into the Community

Healing Circles- Tools for Greater Healing Within a Group Setting

Women's Circles and Men's Circles Separately, Then Together

I believe that bringing the women together first is a huge step towards the ongoing healing process that needs to take place. Women, by cultural teaching and their own natural tendencies are more relational, more readily in tune with their feelings and emotions, and most likely more willing to open up to other women around them. Men also will be much more likely to open up in a safe container of other men first, and then the two sexes can come together. I have two different ideas on how to run these healing circles, though there are of course many more methods, including those that you come up with yourself. The first is an established method of evolutionary healing circles called the Vistar Method. You can find information on this method by looking up the Vistar Foundation on the web at: http://www.vistarfoundation.org.

The "Leaderless Church"

The other is an invention of mine that I like to call the "leaderless church." This model is not really a church per se, but rather an intentional time to come together in healing, share some of the members' talents, and finally to break bread together. To begin, a resonant field is established between the members at the start of the gathering by calling the meeting to order in some way. This sets a strong container for the vulnerability and sharing that will emerge within the energetic space that is created. The space can be set by sharing a visioning exercise, moment of silence, meditation, etc.—basically anything that encourages members to shift themselves from the flurry of their day into the sacred container of the meeting, creating the safe space necessary for the sometimes intense healing work. Really this is just a ritual, similar to that of the processional before a wedding ceremony, designed to create the sacred container in which to have that most life changing moment. It is best to have a practiced spaceholder perform this duty if possible (For more information, See *Holding Space- A Guide to Supporting Others While Remembering to Take Care of Yourself First*, by this author).

After the opening ritual has taken place, the healing work begins. There are different ways to approach this as well, but the main idea is to bring forth everything that needs to be brought to the surface for each of its members. As not all members will have something to offer up on any given day, they may pass if so guided, or bring to the table something from the collective unconscious that they wish to give healing to. Another way to do this is 12-step "check-in'" style, but instead of focusing the meeting on a particular issue that the group is designed around (AA, Al-Anon, etc.), the traumas or hurts brought forth can be in any area of life that each member may have something going on in.

While one person is speaking, all others remain quiet and do not offer condolences or compassion. When the speaker is finished, they indicate this by saying "I'm complete," and then asking for something in that moment from the other members. They may ask for a: prayer, good wishes, positive energy, acknowledgement, or perhaps an apology on behalf of a greater group that one or another of the members may be able to represent (i.e. a person who has been abused by members of another race may ask for a healing apology from others in the group who happen to be of the race that abused that member). Of course the other members do not have to honor the request if they cannot, do not feel guided to, or do not find it in their best interest to do so. However, there will usually be at least one or two people who are in a good enough place to be able to indulge each member in a request for healing, compassion, or apology in one area of life or another, as we all have different wounds.

When every member has gotten a chance to share what was coming up for healing in them that week, the healing circle is closed by a heart-felt wrap up directed by either the facilitator (spaceholder) or one of the members. After the closing of the circle, the room is then re-arranged to allow for the sharing of talents. This is an outlet for people to bring their creativity to others, which is very effective in healing. This is why things such as art therapy, music therapy, and dance therapy exist. In this part of the gathering, members bring forth the creative projects they have been working on to share with the others. It is a "show and tell" or "open mic"' time where people are encouraged to share their art, music, dance, poetry, etc. with the others. This portion of the gathering also serves as a good transition time between the intense healing work and the next portion of the gathering which will include the celebration.

During the last portion of the gathering, members will break bread together by engaging in either a potluck or catered dinner of choice. During this time, everyone is allowed the chance to shift into just being with each other, and additional support can occur between any members who would like to take something from the healing session a bit further. Otherwise, it's a chance to relax and unwind from the sacred space that has been held thus far, and provide a way to ground the intense energy that was created by eating.

In addition to these methods, retreats and other small healing circles can be used in any way that works for those who are in them. Circles can be made up of: all men, all women, women and men, families, children, etc. Just about anything you can imagine can work, though I would advise against bringing forth adult issues in any circles that include children.

How to Promote, Gain Interest in the Circles

Women First

In order to gain interest in these circles, it may be necessary to market them to women at first. You can impress upon women the importance of their "going first" in uncovering the feminine at this time, inspiring them to step into their healing. Let them know that in uncovering their femininity together lies the power to strengthen the feminine and give it a greater chance to be reborn in all of us. The women who are feeling the call and who can no longer sustain the status quo will likely welcome the chance to connect to other women who have also experienced this shift. As most of them will have experienced these shifts, changes, and calls from their inner souls in isolation, a chance to be supported by a group committed to the same personal growth will most likely be an oasis for their souls.

Then the Men

Due to the centuries of cultural repression of embracing the divine feminine in men, in order to market these circles to the vast majority of men—it is going to have to somehow become cool and manly to attend these things. There are two ways to go about this. The first would be by partnering with a few high profile men that other men look to as being an embodiment of "coolness" and getting them to start publicly touting their journey into personal growth and how it is affecting their lives. The second would be by marketing to a core team of conscious, awakened, and committed men who are already in touch with their feminine, or who have been very open to learning through their experiences with women and other keepers of feminine wisdom, who can then begin to affect the male psyche by the ripple effect. In an era when memes and trends can spread and affect the greater psyche in minutes through social media, it is now a lot more possible to sway the masses into signing on to the fact that going to healing circles for men is now cool.

If the previous suggestions are slow to work, there is also another group to market to—those men who are broken down and searching for something new to believe in. They may have followed the prescription of overly masculine paths to happiness and perhaps fought with, competed with, or overpowered their women and found themselves alone and weary—angry at the system for deceiving them, but not quite aware yet of what they can do to reclaim their true inner power to heal themselves and their relationships. I'm sure many of you can come up with all sorts of creative ways to market to these men. They need this healing right now, but will not trust anymore that which is inauthentic. Come up with a way to reach them on their level while coming from love and compassion, and see what emerges. Gear your marketing toward these men in a way that will them excited about matters of the heart. The sacred feminine has been denied them as much as it has been denied women. Come up with ways to get them looking past what culture has set up for them as the ideal of what it means to be a man, and make it cool.

By the law of resonance, and the concept of "when two or more are gathered" from Biblical verse, it has been proven that when we work together on our healing, we have a far greater reach than when we work alone. I would like to conclude this section with the definition of collective resonance from Renee A. Levi, the creator of The Resonance Project: "Collective resonance is, by my definition, a *felt sense of energy, rhythm, or intuitive knowing that occurs in a group of human beings and positively affects the way they interact toward a common purpose.*" (http://www.resonanceproject.org/execsum.cfm)

Resonance then, is at the very essence of using healing circles as tools for healing. It is what expands the reach of our individual, partnership, and family work, and allows for the healing to spread like wildfire to the greater consciousness.

Conclusion

Building the New World

While we are building the world we wish to see (the new paradigm), we still have to survive in the physical reality the way it exists currently (the old paradigm). This polarity is one of the most difficult to reconcile. Whether we are trying to manifest something in our personal world, a new paradigm for the society we live in, or an entirely new world, the "in-between" is a difficult place to navigate.

In these times, it is best to focus on the new that we are building, rather than the old that is falling away. We must give our energy and time to what we envision rather than what is no longer sustainable. We have tried for too long to revive and give new life to the old by attempting change from the outside, in. The only way we will forge ahead into a sustainable future in both our inner and outer landscapes is to begin the change within—for the world outside is truly a reflection of our collective inner worlds.

So what are some concrete ways we can use to cope with the period of transition, when the new has not yet arrived on the outside, but on the inside we are primed and overly ready to live in a world that reflects our new vibration? This is not simple, for sure, but there are things we can do to cultivate and maintain this state of love and healing for ourselves during this time. We can surround ourselves with the things that will keep us in that higher vibration—join spiritual/mindfulness groups, find like-minded friends, journal, meditate, get and do energy work for ourselves, be out in nature and experience the feminine energy often, experience as many beautiful things as we can, work with a life coach, create something, and just "be." We can also remind ourselves often that the change begins within each one of us. It's time to be unafraid of the quiet and stillness required to begin that quest, and begin the journey into our inner worlds, knowing that we are each worthy of a life in vibration with the higher field of LOVE.

About the Author

Amanda Dobra Hope, D.HLc., M.Div., serves the world as an author, speaker, holistic life coach, guide, evolutionary, and healer. A strong desire to search for underlying truth in all situations was a trait that guided her from a very young age. As one who could always see the "elephant in the room," she had the innate knowing that to bring it to the light and do the necessary inner work to release it could bring closer, intimate, and much more satisfying relationships between people. While continually doing her own inner-work, she eventually learned that rather than pointing out what everyone needed to look at in order to free themselves from the emotional bondage she could see that they were in, she could instead strengthen herself in order to be able to hold space properly for those who desired her assistance in order to guide them to their own inner truth.

A huge proponent of "doing the inner work," Amanda's teachings speak to the necessity of personal growth work in order to allow healthier relationships with yourself and others, as well as to inspire and affect those around you—ultimately causing a ripple effect out into the world. She speaks and writes on topics such as: authenticity, how to effectively hold space for yourself and others, how to find your authentic self and live your life in alignment with it, and the healing of the masculine and feminine both as energies as well as how our physiological embodiment affects the way we navigate the world we live in. Find her at: www.itsasyoulikeit.com.

If you enjoyed this book or other titles by this author and believe that they will benefit others, a review on your favorite book-related online site is kindly appreciated.

Connect with me here: www.itsasyoulikeit.com

www.facebook.com/itsasyoulikeit

www. twitter.com/amandadobrahope

www.instagram.com/amandadobrah

www.youtube.com- Search: Amanda Dobra Hope

www.amandadobrahope.wordpress.com

Sign up for my newsletter for information about new books, classes, workshops, speaking engagements, and more! http://eepurl.com/bsKPij

Also by Amanda Dobra Hope

Holding Space- A Guide to Supporting Others While Remembering to Take Care of Yourself First

Do you know what it means to Hold Space? Many people don't, though most people have done it at least a handful of times in their lives. Others may have a special talent for holding space, but don't even realize that's what they are doing since the term is not in popular use yet. This book first defines and clarifies what is meant by the term Holding Space, and then takes the reader on a journey through the life of a spaceholder (one who holds space). The journey will cover initial stirrings of awareness, spiritual considerations and self-care, as well as holding space in relationships, in business, for your dreams, and for the world at large. You will learn where in your life you are already holding space, and how to honor yourself for very beneficial service you are providing. Most importantly, you will learn how to honor your own needs and boundaries first, so that you can be of even greater service to yourself and the world around as you hold space either personally, or professionally.

Life Salad- Everyday Keys to Finding and Living Your Inner Truth
A quippy, practical pocket guide to peeling back the layers of the proverbial onion skin in order to discover who we really are.

Written in language that will capture the reader's attention, and filled with easy to understand concepts, this book presents the reader with an opportunity to look beyond what they've been told or sold to find and fully embrace their unique gifts and talents.

With topics such as: relationships, rituals, surrendering to the flow of life, and energy, there is something for everyone who is interested in simplifying their life and learning how to tune into their inner guidance. This book serves as a fun and practical tool for both beginners as well as more advanced students of their own inner selves.

Made in the USA
Columbia, SC
02 January 2023